The Architecture of

EDWIN LUNDIE

*Publication of this book was supported in part by the Elmer L. and
Eleanor J. Andersen Publications Endowment Fund of the Minnesota Historical Society
and by funds provided by the following generous donors:*

Mr. and Mrs. John H. Daniels

Mr. and Mrs. W. John Driscoll

Martha Sweatt Reed

The Family of Dorothy H. Thompson and the
descendants of James S. Thompson, Sr.

Mr. and Mrs. Frederick T. Weyerhaeuser

The Architecture of
EDWIN LUNDIE

DALE MULFINGER

Foreword by David Gebhard

Essay by Eileen Michels

Minnesota Historical Society Press · St. Paul

Minnesota Historical Society Press
St. Paul 55102

"In Conversation with Mr. Lundie" is reprinted with permission from *Northwest Architect*, May-June 1969, p. 20-21.

This publication is printed on a coated paper manufactured on an acid-free base to ensure long life.

Printed in Canada
10 9 8 7 6 5 4 3 2 1

International Standard Book Number
0-87351-313-4 Cloth
0-87351-314-2 Paper

Library of Congress Cataloging-in-Publication Data
Mulfinger, Dale, 1943-
       The architecture of Edwin Lundie / Dale Mulfinger ; foreword by
   David Gebhard ; essay by Eileen Michels.
           p. cm.
       Includes index.
       ISBN 0-87351-313-4 (cloth). — ISBN 0-87351-314-2 (paper)
       1. Lundie, Edwin Hugh, 1886-1972. 2. Architects—United States—
   Biography. I. Michels, Eileen. II. Title.
   NA737.L86M86 1995
   720'.92—dc20   95-15039

Contents

Foreword

Edwin Lundie and His Contemporaries

DAVID GEBHARD

On first encounter, the houses and other designs of Minnesota architect Edwin H. Lundie would appear to fit comfortably into twentieth-century Period Revivalism. As with other Period Revivalists, he had recourse to such traditional architectural images as the Anglo-Colonial, as well as the French Norman and English Cotswold Cottage, all standard idioms for American architects of this era. Like them his interest in the traditional was essentially in its vernacular, picturesque, and romantic qualities. There is an overriding quality present in his buildings, however, which sets many of them apart from the norm of these years.

Lundie employed a continual reference to the primitive, a quality found in the work of a small number of European and American designers of the nineteenth and twentieth centuries. A reliance on elemental geometric forms, defined by simple surfaces of natural materials—stone, brick, and wood—established this atmosphere of the primitive, which Lundie sophisticatedly maneuvered to intensify the feeling. This sense can effectively be experienced in his details and breakdown of forms in such designs as that for the Shields house at Dellwood (1939–44), the Weed house at White Bear Lake (1939–40), and in his many cabins and summer houses along the North Shore of Lake Superior.

A somewhat older figure who shared this sense of the primitive with Lundie was the respected Beaux-Arts New York architect, Ernest Flagg. In 1922 Flagg published a fascinating volume of text and drawings entitled *Small Houses: Their Economic Design and Construction*. Flagg wrote that his "aim has been to begin at the foundation . . . to use simple and primitive forms and methods, with the hope that they may commend themselves, and prove a new basis in house design." In the chapters that followed, he set down the principles of design necessary to realize "primitive forms and methods." Like many other designers of this century, his principal theme was simplicity, which he extolled by noting that "When the means are simple, there is less chance for concealment, one stands in the open." He then emphasized the need for contrast, which "is of the very essence of design . . . and should always be employed if full values are to be brought out." Of symmetry he observed, "Beyond a certain point, symmetry palls. The beauty of symmetry is heightened by contrast with the lack of it." He concluded with the comment that every successful building must convey "certainty in design."[1]

Flagg's concept of the primitive was not expressed through crudeness or awkwardness. Rather, it relied on a conscious return by the architect to the elemental, pristine forms of structures of the remote and far distant past. The houses presented in Flagg's volume are, on the surface, hardly what one would expect of a Beaux-Arts architect. The design of his houses indeed conveyed a strong sense of the primitive, realized not through an abundance of picturesque details but through the employment of elemental volumes defined by simple unadorned surfaces.

For Lundie and his contemporaries the historic precedent for this recourse to primitive simplicity tempered by a fondness for elementary geometric forms occurred in the late eighteenth and early ninteenth centuries in the designs of Jean-Jacques Le Queu, Joseph M. Gandy, and others. In the nineteenth century, this style turned to and embraced various regional and national vernaculars. Two English examples of primitivism would be Augustus Welby Northmore Pugin's own house at Ramsgate (1843–44) and Philip Webb and William Morris's Red House (1859–60) at Bexleyheath. For nineteenth-century America, the high point of the primitive was reached in the work of Henry Hobson Richardson, especially his Ames Gate Lodge (1880–81) at North Easton, Massachussetts.

Lundie and his colleagues looked to the late nineteenth-century Shingle style for a direct visual and ideological source for their work in the twentieth century. From the 1880s on, the architectural vocabulary of the primitive, geometric, and vernacular emerged as salient ingredients of the Shingle style, particularly in the work of the San Francisco Bay Region architects: Ernest A. Coxhead, Willis Polk, and the younger Bernard R. Maybeck.[2] As with Pugin's, Webb and Morris's, and Richardson's earlier exercises, the designs of these architects suggested but did not in fact embrace any singular vernacular mode, whether Anglo-Colonial, English Cotswold Cottage, or French Norman.

Allusion to one or another (or a combination of several) vernacular traditions was essential to the European, English, and American Arts and Crafts movements. The vernacular picturesque tradition also served as a principal source for the Period Revival from the early 1900s through the 1940s. Certainly in America, most examples of the Anglo-Colonial Revival or the vernacular French or English medieval prior to 1920 were loose in their historic imagery and, in many instances, highly inventive in their interpretation of architectural precedent. Less frequent were the direct or even low-keyed references in examples of Period Revivalism to the play between the primitive and the geometric.

As was the case with Lundie at a later date, there was a small but influential group of American architects who advocated a return to primitive elements of design during the first decades of the century. Among these designers were such figures as the Pittsburgh architect Benno Jenssen, the California architect Charles F. Whittlesey, and the New York architects, Lewis Colt Albro, Grosvenor Atterbury, and Harrie T. Lindeberg.[3] The work of all of these architects was widely published in the principal architectural journals of their time and in the pages of upper-middle-class shelter magazines.

The similarity of approach between Lundie and Atterbury is evident in the latter architect's ability to abstract and return to the primitive. This can be seen in Atterbury's resort to the Moorish tradition in his 1897 Havemeyer house on Long Island; to the rural rustic in his James house of 1916 at Newport, Rhode

Island; or to the vernacular Hispanic in the Pond house of 1936 in Tucson, Arizona. Lindeberg's urge to the primitive underlay his design for the Neuhaud house of 1923 in Houston; his own house of 1924 in Locust Valley, Long Island; and the Patterson house of 1925 in Dayton, Ohio.[4] Of these architects, it was Benno Jenssen who came the closest to Lundie, especially in his well-publicized country house for Edgar J. Kaufmann near Pittsburgh (1924–26).[5]

The idea of abstracting one or another of the historic traditions (and on occasion making reference to the primitive) continued into the 1920s. The general tendency of Period Revival architects was to rely on the openly picturesque, which more often than not was realized by a rich array of handcrafted details. The goal, particularly in domestic architecture, was to create houses and their accompanying gardens that expressed charm, romance, atmosphere, and personality.

For those designers such as Lundie, the qualities of charm and open romance were at best marginal. What counted for them was a building that looked to the primitive to establish its atmosphere and above all its character and personality. If the sense of romance (of the distant past) was present, it was filtered through the subtle expression of elemental geometric forms.

In California the urge to return to historic, simple, picturesque, and romantic vernacular forms followed a course similar to that pursued by Lundie. The Andalusian-inspired houses of George Washington Smith of Santa Barbara and of Clarence A. Tantau of San Francisco perfectly match the approach taken by Lundie.[6] Like Lundie's work, Smith's painterly designs, such as his Andalusian Baldwin house of 1925 in San Marino or his Byzantine-inspired Crocker-Fagan house of 1926–28 at Pebble Beach, suggested a possible bridge (with its emphatic geometric forms) between the use of primitive forms and the then-developing modern. Tantau's Armsby ranch house of 1928–29 at Carmel-by-the-Sea employed rough native stone for the unadorned walls of its flat-, shed-, and gable-roofed volumes. The Armsby house comes close to evoking the picturesque, but it certainly is not charming or romantic, at least in the 1920s sense of these terms.[7]

Turning to the Midwest, Lundie's own territory, the Chicago architects David Adler and his younger colleague Jerome Robert Cerny both occasionally had recourse to the primitive in their work. In the case of Adler, reductionism is evident in his Italian-precedent Hamills house (1928) and in his Georgian Wheeler house (1934)—both in Lake Forest, Illinois.[8] Jerome Robert Cerny came close at times in his simplification of historic forms to his contemporary Lundie. Like Lundie he, on occasion, combined a medieval and Anglo-Colonial Revival image in a single design, for instance, in his Warren house (1954) in Farmington, Virginia.[9] A close look at Lundie's Colonial Revival Sweatt house (1947–56) at Lake Minnetonka and Cerny's Warren house illustrates how both of these architects thought in terms of assembled fragments and exaggerated features, such as chimneys.

The one geographic region where a number of designers produced work similar to Lundie's was the Pacific Northwest—George Wellington Stoddard and Lionel H. Pries in Seattle and Wade Pipes, Harold W. Doty, Albert E. Doyle, and especially Herman Brookman in Portland.[10] The tendency of these designers was to use several historic images within a single design, much as Lundie did. The most frequent combination was the rustic informal Craftsman house coupled with a hint of the English or French medieval, along with a few details and references to the Anglo-Colonial Revival. Of the Portland designs, Herman Brookman's work came closest to that of Lundie. Brookman's Green house (1926) in Portland suggests the Late Medieval Tudor, more in the sense of returning to a primitive beginning rather than being a correct historical interpretation.[11] Equally difficult to pin down historically are such later, lightly medieval houses of Brookman such as the Greene house (1933) or the Baruh (Zell) house (1936)—both in Portland.[12] Like Lundie he used the Colonial theme loosely, as in his Lewis house (1937) in Portland.[13]

One figure who formed a connective link between the northern Pacific Coast and the Upper Midwest was William Gray Purcell. Purcell's early Prairie School work (accomplished with his partners George Grant Elmslie and George Feick, Jr.) in and around Minneapolis and St. Paul was well known to architects in the area. After World War I Purcell moved to Portland and established his practice. He quickly encompassed the primitive reductionism of the locale in his own house (1920) and in his Bell house (1927). In the late 1920s, he brought this northwest mode back to Minneapolis in his Peterson house (1927–28) and in several of his speculative houses built in southwest Minneapolis (1928).

Thus Lundie's continual use of the Anglo-Colonial Revival image in many of his designs essentially mirrored the way the image was used throughout the country, from the early 1920s through the post–World War II years. Lundie's most successful Anglo-Colonial Revival interpretations fall into the category referred to in the 1920s and 1930s as the "Early American Farm House style" or as the "Free rendering of the Colonial Style."[14] These same labels could be applied to the designs of Dwight James Baum and Roger C. Bullard and above all to some of the designs of the highly popular Boston architect, Royal Barry Wills.[15] Wills's well-publicized 1939 *Life Magazine*-sponsored house for the Blackbourn family in Edina, Minnesota, reinforced a mode that already enjoyed great favor in the Twin Cities.[16] As with many of Lundie's Colonial designs of the 1930s and later, Wills's Blackbourn house expressed a loose interpretation of a Cape Cod cottage. (It was not "correct" as was often the case with Wills's classic Colonial designs.)

In the post–World War II American architectural scene, there was no one who really paralleled the primitive approach to design still pursued by Lundie. Triumphant modernists, such as Marcel L. Breuer and even on occasion Philip C. Johnson, might employ rustic masonry chimneys and podiums, but these forms referred to the world of rectilinear geometry, rather than to the primitive. On the West Coast, San Francisco's Third Bay Tradition abstractly played with the earlier wood vernacular traditions, but again their results were not meant to suggest a return to primitive beginnings.

In spite of abstracting traditional forms, the post–1945 designs of Wills and of Cerny had far different results. Their many Colonial designs continued to express the ideals of charm and historic romanticism, coupled with indirect references to the then-popular modern. Their strongest primitive designs (as was the case in their pre–World War II work) were always found in those houses that were historically accurate renditions of seventeenth- and early eighteenth-century vernacular forms of New England. Neither Lundie nor his clients generally seemed interested in such open historical references. Historical references for them were to be found in fragmented details—a fireplace mantel, a side-lighted and fan-lighted entrance doorway, or even via a single volume. But the building as a whole was never an outright correct historic version of the Anglo-Colonial or of medieval English or French vernacular architecture.

Lundie's lakeshore houses and cottages are also unique in the post–World War II years. There were plenty of simple woodsy recreational houses and cottages built across the country during these years, but their architectural sources were almost always the vernacular or do-it-yourselfism, not the primitive. In striking contrast to Lundie's designs, these other structures radiate charm and vernacular romance but not a feeling for the primitive.

In the end, Lundie's work impressively fulfills several of the essential qualities sought by traditionalist architects—of expressing romance, character, and personality via direct and indirect references to architectural images of the past. Lundie's aesthetic determination to revert to an atmosphere of primitive beginnings resulted in a set of strong, unique buildings. He had a remarkable ability to suggest the past via Colonial Revival, medieval, and Scandinavian images but at the same time to make these images highly personal. No matter what its historic source might be, a Lundie building is easily recognizable. He, indeed, was able to realize the traditionalist ideal of imparting character and personality through his designs.

NOTES

1. Ernest Flagg, *Small Houses: Their Economic Design and Construction* (New York: Charles Scribner's Sons, 1922), 52, 118, 136, 144, 146. For more on Flagg, see Adolf K. Placzek, ed., *Macmillan Encyclopedia of Architects* (New York: Macmillan Pub. Co., Free Press, 1982), 2:87–89; Henry F. Withey and Elsie Rathburn Withey, *Biographical Dictionary of American Architects (Deceased)* (Los Angeles: Hennessy & Ingalls, Inc., 1970), 211–12.

2. Sally Woodbridge, ed., with an introduction by David Gebhard, *Bay Area Houses* (New York: Oxford University Press, 1976; Salt Lake City: Peregrine Smith Books, 1988); Richard W. Longstreth, *On the Edge of the World: Four Architects in San Francisco at the Turn of the Century* (New York: Architectural History Foundation; Cambridge: MIT Press, 1983).

3. Benno Jenssen was educated in St. Louis, worked in the Boston office of Shepley, Rutan and Coolidge, and later attended the École des Beaux-Arts in Paris. For an example of the work of Jenssen, see Augusta Own Patterson, "The Rolling Rock Club in Pennsylvania," *Town and Country*, May 15, 1931, p. 53–60. For Whittlesey and Colt, see Withey and Withey, *Biographical Dictionary*, 655–56, 12–13. For examples of Whittlesey's work, see "Reinforced Concrete Construction—Why I Believe in It," *Architect and Engineer*, Mar. 1908, p. 37–57. For examples of Colt's and Lindeberg's early work, see C. Matlack Price, "The Recent Work of Albro and Lindeberg," *Architecture*, Jan. 1915, p. 1–39. For Atterbury, see Placzek, ed., *Macmillan Encyclopedia*, 1:113–14. For a presentation of his early work, see C. Matlack Price, "The Development of a National Architecture: The Work of Grosvenor Atterbury," *Arts and Decoration* 2, no. 5 (Mar. 1912): 176–79. For an expression of his views on design, see John Taylor Boyd, Jr., "Personality in Architecture: An Interview with Grosvenor Atterbury," *Arts and Decoration* 32, no. 6 (Apr. 1930): 49–52, 92. Harrie T. Lindeberg (1880–1959) received his architectural training in the office of McKim, Mead and White,

established his own practice in New York in 1906, and a few years later associated with Lewis Colt Albro. For Albo and Lindeberg's designs, see Lewis Colt Albro and Harrie T. Lindeberg, *Domestic Architecture* (New York: Privately printed, 1912); for Lindeberg's later work, see Harrie T. Lindeberg, *Domestic Architecture of H. T. Lindeberg* (New York: W. Helburn, 1940). For Lindeberg's views of design, see John Taylor Boyd, Jr., "Modern Architecture That is Not Modernistic," *Arts and Decoration* 31, no. 5 (Sept. 1929): 48–52, 92, 94, 96, 100.

4. Probably known to Edwin Lundie was Lindeberg's 1918 house for John S. Pillsbury at Lake Minnetonka, Minnesota.

5. The Kaufmann house, La Torelle, was illustrated in *Country Life,* July 1928, p. 57–60. In 1936 Kaufmann commissioned Frank Lloyd Wright to design the famed weekend house, Fallingwater, at Bear Run, Pa.

6. For Smith, see Placzek, ed., *Macmillan Encyclopedia,* 4:88–89; David Gebhard, *George Washington Smith, 1876–1930: The Spanish Colonial Revival in California* (Santa Barbara: University of California, 1964). For Smith's admiration for the primitive, see John Taylor Boyd, Jr., "Houses Showing a Distingished Simplicity: An Interview with George Washington Smith," *Arts and Decoration* 33, no. 6 (Oct. 1930): 57–60, 112.

7. For Tantau, see Withey and Withey, *Biographical Dictionary,* 589–90. For the Armsby house, see *California Arts and Architecture,* Apr. 1930, p. 43–46. For other examples of Tantau's work, see Mary Kellogg, "Three California Houses Designed by Clarence A. Tantau," *House Beautiful* 66, no. 1 (July 1929): 52–53, 90.

8. For Adler, see Withey and Withey, *Biographical Dictionary,* 10–11. For Adler's work, see Richard Pratt, *David Adler: The Architect and His Work* (New York: M. Evans and Co., 1970). Adler's design for the Hamills house was that of an extensive addition and remodeling of an earlier house.

9. Jerome Robert Cerny (b. 1901) studied at the Royal Academy in London, at the École des Beaux-Arts, and for a period at the American Academy in Rome. He opened his architectural practice in Chicago in 1930. For more on his work, see *A Monograph of Country Houses: Robert Jerome Cerny Architect* (Chicago: Privately published, [1955?]).

10. George McMath, "A Regional Style Comes to the City," in Thomas Vaughan and Virginia Guest Ferriday, ed., *Space, Style and Structure: Building in Northwest America* (Portland: Oregon Historical Society, 1974), 467–508.

11. "The Residence of Harry A. Green, Portland, Oregon; Herman Brookman, Architect," *Architecture* 58:3 (Sept. 1928): 165–69.

12. "Portland Can Boast a Variety of Architecture," *House and Garden,* Dec. 1934, p. 46–49; "House for Mr. & Mrs. Leo Baruh, Portland, Oregon; Hollis Johnson and Herman Brookman, Architects," *Architect and Engineer,* May 1939, p. 36.

13. "Small House for Mr. & Mrs. R. P. Lewis, Portland; Hollis Johnson and Herman Brookman, Architects," *Architect and Engineer,* May 1939, p. 36.

14. The subject of the various Colonal styles was extensively discussed, especially during the 1920s and 1930s. See Henry Humphrey, Jr., "What Type of House Shall I Build? I. The Colonial House," *Country Life* 48, no. 6 (Oct. 1925): 61–63; John Normile, *New Ideas: The Architectural Forum Book of Small Houses* (New York: Simon and Schuster, 1938), xxxiv.

15. David Gebhard, "The American Colonial Revival of the 1930s," *Winterthur Portfolio* 22, no. 2/3 (Summer/Autumn 1987): 109–48.

16. David Gebhard, "Royal Barry Wills and the American Colonial Revival," *Winterthur Portfolio* 27, no. 1 (Spring 1992): 45–74.

Acknowledgments

Research for this study was supported by the Department of Architecture, University of Minnesota; the Graham Foundation; the Research Department of the Minnesota Historical Society; and the Northwest Architectural Archives, University of Minnesota.

I wish to extend special thanks to the tireless work of researchers Leffert Tigelaar, Cheryl Fosdick, and the many students of the Edwin Lundie research seminars.

Thanks also must go to Scott Berry, Tom Martinson, and Simon Beeson for their support of research and ideas for this project. Both Alan K. Lathrop and Barbara Bezat of the Northwest Architectural Archives gave willing support and cheerful assistance, especially with Lundie's drawings. Peter Kerze deserves special recognition for his excellent color photography of Lundie buildings.

I am particularly pleased that my editor Sally Rubinstein at the Minnesota Historical Society Press rendered my words intelligible. Jean Brookins, Ann Regan, Alan Ominsky, and Nordis Heyerdahl-Fowler at the Press also helped make this book a beautiful reality. Designer Lois Stanfield gave the benefit of her artistic eye to every page layout.

I am grateful for the gracious consideration by current and past owners of Lundie designs who have shared their homes with this roving vagabond and who now make it possible for others to enjoy Lundie's creations. May all who read this book respect their privacy.

My apologies go to Kira and Anna for the lack of attention from their loving dad, who all too often escaped to Lundie hunts and later to Lundie writing.

And to Jan I dedicate this book in appreciation for her unending support in my consuming quest of architecture.

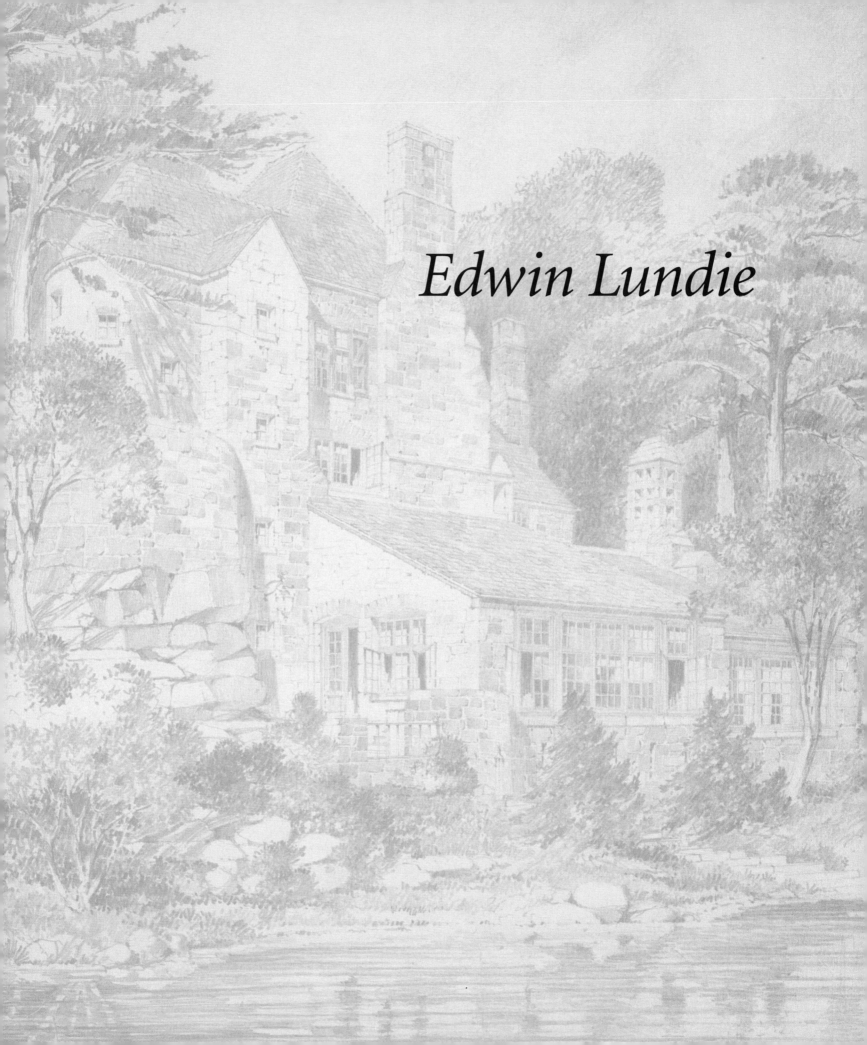

Edwin Lundie

Edwin Lundie, 1886–1972

EILEEN MICHELS

Edwin Hugh Lundie was born in Cedar Rapids, Iowa, on October 13, 1886, to Samuel and Emma Lenore Hitchcock Lundie.[1] He attended Polk and Jackson grade schools in Cedar Rapids between 1892 and 1899, and, after the family left Iowa, high school in Salem, South Dakota, from 1900 to 1903.[2] By 1906 Samuel Lundie had moved to Campbell in west-central Minnesota where he carried on a farmland real estate business, and about 1912 he moved to St. Paul and opened a real estate office. In later life Lundie recalled that his family supplied him with reading materials that fired his imagination and left a lifelong taste for books and literature. He was particularly close to his grandfather, Lucius Edwin Hitchcock, and in later years often acknowledged his formative influence.

Lundie was listed for the first time in the St. Paul city directory in 1906 as a stock clerk for Farwell, Ozman, Kirk and Company, a hardware wholesaler.[3] However, by the next year, when he was twenty-one and listed as a draftsman for Louis Lockwood, a relatively undistinguished St. Paul architect, he had set out to become an architect.

What force propelled Lundie to architecture remains unknown. His daughter could recall only that he knew from an early age that he wanted to be an architect.[4] In 1961, at the age of seventy-five, Lundie reflected publicly on the beginning of his long career. He recalled that he first became a student, that is presumably an unpaid apprentice, and then an employee of Cass Gilbert, then an employee of Thomas Holyoke, and after that an employee of Emmanuel Masqueray. Memories are not infallible, and the historical record changes and amplifies his recollection.

Although Lundie was never listed in the city directory as a student or employee of Cass Gilbert (1858–1934), Gilbert nevertheless played a part in Lundie's development. Gilbert's own architectural education, gained during a four-year period between 1876 and 1880, had been a combination of several elements not unusual for the time: office boy, apprenticeship, self-study, and brief formal academic training at the Massachusetts Institute of Technology, topped off with a few months of European travel and sketching and subsequent employment in the New York firm of McKim, Mead and White. Thus Gilbert had gained practical experience and been introduced to the prevailing American architectural scene, to some of the highlights of European architecture, and, of great importance, to the architectural curriculum at MIT, the first such academic education in the United States. A predilection for the precepts of classicism as formulated at the École des Beaux-Arts in Paris prevailed at MIT. The development of a rich, neo-Baroque architectural mode, now variously called Beaux-Arts, eclecticism, or academicism, swept the country by the mid-1890s and also became the basis of Gilbert's mature style.

Gilbert opened an architectural practice in St. Paul in 1883 shortly after returning to the city where he had grown up. He first gained national attention in 1895 as the designer of the Minnesota State Capitol and, a few years later, as the architect of several important commercial buildings in New York. By the time Lundie arrived in St. Paul, Gilbert was primarily cultivating an eastern clientele and spending as much time in New York as in St. Paul; he had opened an office in New York in 1900 and listed that city as his residence in 1903.

The assumption has been that between 1900 and 1910, when Gilbert closed his St. Paul office, he and Thomas Holyoke (1876–1925) worked together in a partnership. Actually, after 1900, Holyoke, a St. Paul native who also had briefly been a student in Paris as well as a draftsman for Gilbert from 1884 to about 1891 and then again from 1896 through 1899, carried on an independent practice in Gilbert's St. Paul office until 1910. During those years of sharing office space with Gilbert, Holyoke no doubt from time to time attended to certain aspects of Gilbert's dwindling midwestern practice.

At no time was Lundie listed as a student or employee of Gilbert, but he was listed as a draftsman for Holyoke from 1908 through 1912. While an employee of Holyoke, Lundie would have seen very little of Gilbert, who by that time was rarely in the St. Paul office. Nevertheless, Gilbert's fleeting visits and the valuable wealth of books and drawings still available in the shared office until 1910 left a deep impression on Lundie. Years later Lundie praised Gilbert's dedication, hard work, force of character, and abhorrence of sloppy workmanship—professional traits that clients would in turn come to value in Lundie.[5] He also recalled studying design, detail, and drawing in Gilbert's office and perusing its architectural books. Not least in importance, Lundie, who always loved to draw, responded directly and positively to Gilbert's accomplished renderings.

When Lundie came into the Holyoke office, apprenticeship via the office draftsman route was still a common, acceptable way of entering the profession, even though many universities had by then established academic architectural programs similar to the one at MIT. It would be several more decades before a four-year university architectural education became the norm.

In later years Lundie recalled, erroneously, that he became a draftsman for Emmanuel Masqueray (1861–1917) in 1911 and attended Atelier Masqueray from 1911 to 1914. He was listed in the city directory as a draftsman in the office of Emmanuel L. Masqueray from 1913 through 1915. Masqueray, born in France

Office of Masqueray, who is seated third from left; Lundie is behind Masqueray's left shoulder. Percell Haskins, Masqueray's valet, stands at far left; the other persons are unidentified (ca. 1914).

and trained at the École des Beaux-Arts, which had provided the model for the MIT curriculum, had subsequently worked for Carrere and Hastings, Richard Morris Hunt, and Warren and Wetmore, all skillful New York practitioners of Beaux-Arts classicism. He also established Atelier Masqueray in New York in 1892, a teaching studio patterned after Beaux-Arts ateliers in Paris.

Masqueray first gained widespread recognition as the chief designer of the Louisiana Purchase Exposition in St. Louis in 1904. His designs for the St. Louis fair were akin to those of the World's Columbian Exposition held in Chicago in 1893, an event that had widely popularized Beaux-Arts architecture.

At that exposition, he met Archbishop John Ireland, a forceful Roman Catholic cleric who was seeking an architect to design an architecturally imposing new cathedral for St. Paul. Masqueray produced an acceptable design for it in 1905 and, encouraged by Archbishop Ireland, shortly thereafter moved to St. Paul.[6] For the rest of his life he specialized in ecclesiastical design, primarily for clients throughout the Midwest. In addition to the St. Paul Cathedral, notable Twin Cities examples are the Basilica of St. Mary in Minneapolis and the 1909 Church of St. Louis and the 1915 Chapel at the University of St. Thomas, both in St. Paul.

In 1906 he also established a St. Paul version of Atelier Masqueray, which was affiliated with the Society of Beaux-Arts Architects. Among Lundie's papers is a four-page brochure, *Circular of Information Concerning the Educational Work of the Society of Beaux-Arts Architects for Its Twentieth Season,* describing the educational goals of the society and explaining the complicated, rigidly uniform system of design competitions to be conducted during the 1912–13 competition season by all of the society's ateliers then springing up throughout the country. Competition design problems were for imaginary exalted public building types similar to those given out for the École des Beaux-Arts *concours.* They had little to do with the more mundane realities of most American architectural practice. Considering his packrat tendencies to save all kinds of things that were meaningful to him, the single brochure in his papers suggests that he was one of Atelier Masqueray's students only during the 1912–13 competition year.

There are a few early Lundie drawings of architectural details of the sort expected of atelier students. They are not very good, however, and hindsight suggests that his talents and Beaux-Arts atelier methodology were incompatible.

From the 1870s until about 1920, local architectural clubs, far less formal in nature than the ateliers, were additional avenues of architectural self-education for aspiring apprentices and draftsmen. Established architects lectured about the nature and history of architecture, taught design, and judged design and rendering competitions. Lundie was one of eight young men who founded the Gargoyle Club in St. Paul on January 13, 1913.[7] A perspective rendering labeled Farm House Competition, signed "Edwin H. Lundie, Architect" and published in the *Minnesota Farmers' Library* in April 1914 is typical of the practical types of buildings that were club competition subjects.

Each week Lundie spent five long days and Saturday until noon in the office and studied evenings and weekends at the St. Paul School of Art, the Gargoyle Club, and Atelier Masqueray. During his years of study and work at close hand with two important architects and at some remove with an illustrious third, Lundie matured as an architect. Later he said that he could not have received a

One of Lundie's pencil drawings of classical architectural details (undated)

EDWIN H LUNDIE. ARCHITECT.
ST. PAUL.

Farm house competition drawing done in pencil. Frank Abrahamson and Magnus Jemne also entered designs in the 1913 competition.

finer education in any architectural school in the country.[8] He simultaneously developed practical as well as theoretical and artistic skills, and along the way he became a superb perspective renderer, a true artist of the genre. In fact, in 1916 and 1917 Lundie was listed in the city directory as a draftsman without office affiliation, suggesting that he earned a living as a free-lance draftsman or delineator. If that is the case, he was continuing the nineteenth-century tradition of so-called architect's artists, that is free-lance renderers who worked for different architects as needed.

Masqueray died in May 1917. The next month Lundie and two of his former colleagues from Masqueray's office, Fred Slifer (1885–1948) and Frank Abrahamson (1883–1972), signed a copartnership agreement establishing the firm of Slifer, Lundie, and Abrahamson, housed in the Endicott Building, in order to finish Masqueray's thirteen uncompleted commissions, which were collectively worth $22,710, a not insubstantial sum for the day.[9] Each partner was to receive thirty-five dollars per week and share equally in any profits or losses. Majority decisions would prevail in the conduct of the office business, but each would assume sole architectural responsibility for a certain number of the unfinished projects. Lundie, then thirty-one years old and trained by an arduous ten-year course of self-study and employment, was at last able to function as an equal in a partnership of three.

Pen-and-ink perspective rendering of the Cathedral of St. Joseph, Sioux Falls, South Dakota (1918)

He also felt able to support a wife, and he and Grace Halroyd Nash were married on October 17, 1917. Grace Nash, one of two daughters of Percy and Sarah Nash, both English immigrants, was born in St. Paul in 1891 and educated at St. Joseph's Academy. Lundie considered her his greatest ally and severest critic, and she was his constant helpmate. Their only child, Ellen, born in 1920, described her mother as a physically slight woman of innate good taste, a devoted wife content to live in the shadow of a husband who was completely absorbed in his profession.[10]

Among the important unfinished Masqueray projects that Lundie oversaw were the design of the high altar and the remaining construction for the Chapel of the College of St. Thomas; the St. Paul Seminary grotto; the Cathedral in Sioux Falls, South Dakota; and the Church of St. Louis in Turton, South Dakota.

Since the perspective rendering of the Sioux Falls Cathedral bears Lundie's signature as renderer but Masqueray's name as architect, it seems likely that this stylistically eclectic but skillfully handled design, which in massing resembles the Cathedral of St. Paul, is Masqueray's concept. Lundie probably supervised the completion of the project and designed numerous articles of church furniture, which are in a late medieval style. However, the drawings for the church in

Turton bear the label of Slifer, Lundie, and Abrahamson, and therefore Lundie probably did the design as well as the rendering. It is a fanciful Late Gothic Revival design, resembling the equally imaginative medieval pastiches of Ralph Adams Cram (1863–1942) and Bertram Goodhue (1869–1924). There is a sense of solid wall rather than of mere masonry skeleton, and its decorative details refer to the lacy intricacies of English Perpendicular or French Flamboyant prototypes.

The partnership of Slifer, Lundie, and Abrahamson was amicably dissolved on June 17, 1919.[11] Lundie received $400.02 or one-third of the $1,200.06 then on hand as profit. He assigned his interest in the office library and architectural plates (presumably architectural photographs and clippings) to the others for another $200.00, and it was agreed that Lundie would complete the parish house and sacristies of the Sioux Falls Cathedral, the Church of St. Louis in Turton, the school building for the parish of Our Lady of Good Counsel in Elkton, South Dakota, and St. John's Church and parish house in Cedar Rapids, Iowa. Lundie kept all of the office drawings pertaining to these unfinished projects, as well as part of the office furniture, some of which remained in his office until his death. Slifer and Abrahamson retained the rest of Masqueray's unfinished commissions along with the drawings for the Cathedral of St. Paul and other churches.

The Slifer, Lundie, and Abrahamson partnership was dissolved because the contacts that Lundie had developed in Sioux Falls led to his first sizable independent commission, the design of a new diocesan college at Sioux Falls. It was enough to launch a solo practice, and he rented office space in the Endicott Building. After years of preparation, Lundie finally was able to begin a truly independent practice in which he was sole principal. It would absorb him for the next five decades.

Over the years, Lundie was approached by other architects who discussed partnership with him. Although no formal partnerships ever materialized, in 1923 Holyoke, then a principal in the firm of Holyoke and Davis, suggested combining office spaces, and Lundie moved into the Holyoke office on December 31, 1923. His portion of the rent was about fifty dollars a month. His papers reveal constant financial pressures and anxieties during the 1920s, and this was an obvious way of reducing office overhead. After Holyoke's death in March 1925, Lundie seemed to be in arrears with his share of the rent more or less constantly through 1929. In 1930 he moved out of the shared space and into Number 324 in the Endicott Building, which remained his office for the rest of his life.

Until 1923 Lundie's practice was primarily in religious and institutional architecture. As is evident in the design for the diocesan college, he was learning to quote the complex, historical modes used by his mentors, although in this instance the finished result is not particularly impressive. The pen-and-ink perspective rendering of the project suggests that he had a more picturesque effect in mind, which was not realized in actuality.

By contrast the 1919 renderings for St. Rita's Academy in Sioux Falls (also called Presentation Academy) show a more irregular, yet more integrated and interesting, design that was stylistically Late Gothic Revival. Aside from minor alterations carried out in 1925 to existing buildings at Macalester College in St. Paul, Lundie did no other designs for educational institutions.

Chapel of the Diocesan College, Sioux Falls, South Dakota (1924)

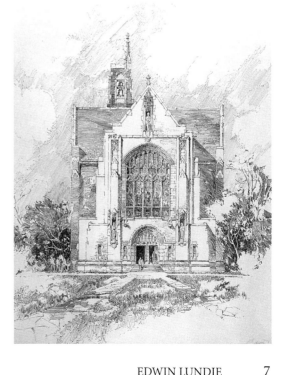

Elevation in pen and ink of St. Rita's Academy, Sioux Falls, South Dakota (1919)

In 1922 Lundie received the commission to design St. Joseph's Hospital in Mitchell, South Dakota. The simple cubic forms, the flat brick walls, and the disciplined neo-Baroque stone entrance recall another historicizing style of the day, the Georgian Revival. Throughout the 1920s he was unsuccessful in attempts to secure other hospital design commissions. However, by the 1940s, when his reputation as a residential architect was secure, he declined the commission offered by the director of St. Joseph's Hospital for a second hospital design and instead suggested another architect.

While the largest of Lundie's nonresidential commissions during the 1920s and 1930s were for Catholic institutions, he also worked on other smaller projects for other denominations. In the 1920s he carried out various alterations to the rectory, church, and parish house of St. Clement's Episcopal Church in St. Paul, an 1894 design by Cass Gilbert. He also did alterations in 1923 for the Lutheran church in Mahtomedi and the First Church of Christ Scientist in nearby White Bear Lake.

The decade of the 1920s was a period of constant hard work and financial anxiety as Lundie struggled to support his family, establish himself professionally, and remodel his own small house in Mahtomedi, which he had bought in 1923.[12] Lundie was determined to be sole principal in a small office. Although he declined all offers of partnership, on occasion when other architects in the Endicott Building were out of town, he supervised their offices. When money was particularly scarce, he did free-lance renderings for other architects in St. Paul and Chicago, charging between $100 and $250 for each of them.

As part of the process of cultivating professional success, Lundie became, to a certain extent, a networking professional and civic joiner. He continued to be active in the Gargoyle Club until 1927 and for years lunched on Thursdays with downtown associates who constituted the informal Why-Name-It Club. In 1922 he joined the American Institute of Architects (AIA), and from then on he was active in affairs of the St. Paul chapter.[13]

Slowly during the 1920s his endeavors built up a clientele of socially prominent St. Paul and White Bear Lake families. During the Great Depression, he managed to keep his business afloat chiefly as a result of several substantial residential commissions from people who had retained their wealth. In 1936 Lundie's fortunes suddenly, substantially, and permanently improved. By 1947 he had a waiting list of clients and actually from time to time turned some away.

Edwin Lundie (left) in his office with two of his employees, Louis Bramstedt (center) and Frank D. Clark (right) in 1969

By choice, he kept his office small, never employing more than five draftsmen at any one time and usually fewer than that.[14] They apparently were hired as needed, even on a week-to-week basis, with few long-term commitments. He was at the boards himself throughout his career and closely oversaw all aspects of a given project; indeed, his personal involvement and exacting standards most likely were the reasons for his thriving practice. Clients knew they would be working with Lundie all the way, not an unknown subordinate. Eventually Lundie set his compensation at 12 percent of cost, plus travel expenses.

After 1923 Lundie increasingly specialized in residential design. He once said that his houses were traditional in style but that they had a romantic quality that made them timeless and imaginative.[15] His ability to infuse new life into a variety of traditional forms was reflected in the citation that accompanied his investiture as a Fellow of the AIA in 1948.

> [Edwin H. Lundie] Admittee to the Institute in 1922, is advanced to Fellowship for his contribution in the field of design. Through his intimate knowledge of the building crafts and his fertile native ability, he has created structures of utility and beauty.[16]

He was aware of modern design currents; his library contained books about modern architects and architecture, and he seemed particularly to save material that debated the relative merits of modernism versus traditionalism. But his own skills lay elsewhere, and as his journals and clippings files make clear, his artistic historicism and eclecticism was a conscious choice. He had important counterparts in every major American city. Banished from the pages of the postwar professional architectural press, which was singlemindedly focused on modernism, to local newspapers and so-called decorator's magazines such as *House and Garden*,[17] Lundie and others like him have been given their rightful places in the historical mainstream only in recent years.

Stylistically, Lundie was not propelled from one project to the next by the artistic momentum of his own developmental phases. Rather, he responded to each client's specific wishes. Like his mentors, Lundie drew intelligently from a broad range of architectural history for design solutions for a given job. Consideration of Lundie's residential architecture involves less a matter of tracing consistent, chartable stylistic change and development from decade to decade, or from one project to the next, than of recognizing a few basic spatial modes or types that he used repeatedly in a variety of situations.

The small, two-story Colonial Revival house of simple rectangular plan, often with a porch or garage added to one side, first appeared in his work in 1922. From then until 1947 a number of them were built in the St. Paul neighborhoods of north St. Anthony Park and the adjacent University Grove area of University of Minnesota faculty housing (see p. 32). Most of them had white, shingle siding and well-detailed, symmetrical fenestration. Most bore the Lundie trademark of a whimsical, cutout shutter design that was individually tailored for each house. Lundie's drawings indicate that no detail of these modest houses was too insignificant for his meticulous attention. Lundie had never traveled in New England but instead absorbed the basic forms and artistic nuances of the Colonial Revival at second hand through books in his library. Time and again throughout his life, the published pictorial image that fed his

Perspective rendering in pencil for a Colonial Revival house for the
University Grove neighborhood in St. Paul (1925)

imagination served as his means of access to distant buildings that he never saw or experienced spatially.

The nicety of proportion, detailing, craftsmanship, materials, and all-around livability of these Colonial Revival designs are instantly appealing. Lundie designed several scaled-down versions of the same form for the Thome Corporation in 1923 and the Weyerhaeuser Corporation in 1937. Even though planned for tightly budgeted speculative construction, they, too, are relatively carefully detailed.

A second type of house design, which also first appeared in the 1920s, became another constant in his repertory. This type involved an asymmetrical accretion of rectangular spatial blocks of varying height and width placed side by side on an unbroken axis or at right angles to each other. Gables, chimneys, secluded

A Lundie design for the Weyerhaeuser Corporation, published in 1940

SIX ROOMS · TWO STORY
PLAN 62-E

ANY ARCHITECT who can develop nine closets in a six room house—and good sized closets too—is bound to produce a very special house. And that is what Mr. Lundie has done. For you see an exceptionally commodious plan, considering it lies within a square space 25′9″ by 25′9″. But all the merit of this house is not on the inside.

This house might be dropped overnight into any of our famous old villages, such as Ridge-field, Conn., and even a native would not sense a jarring note in its facade. Note the distinguished doorway, and exquisitely detailed lantern and downspout. It is by touches such as these that a good house is turned into a distinguished one.

WEYERHAEUSER   4-SQUARE   HOMES

Perspective rendering in pencil of a White Bear Lake cottage (ca. 1926)

Perspective rendering in pencil of a White Bear Lake residence (ca. 1926)

Perspective rendering in pencil, Hermant studio project (1923)

corners, and richly textured wall surfaces added to the picturesque quality, and abundant informal planting was almost always a requisite accompaniment. There was an integral relationship between building and site.

Stylistically some of these picturesque houses refer to American Colonial designs, but often it is difficult to isolate a single historical source. Houses of this type were built throughout the Twin Cities and its suburbs between 1927 and 1954, and, during the 1940s, in Rochester. After 1940, several were built in Florida as winter retreats for Twin Cities clients. One of the most delightful, albeit unexecuted, designs in this picturesque, romantic mode was for a small studio that Warren Hermant, the sculptor who had been associated with Lundie on the decoration of the Sioux Falls projects, commissioned in 1923 for a site in southern France near Monte Carlo. It was one of Lundie's favorite projects.

In 1925 Lundie did the first of the large residences for country estates located on suburban lakeshore or river sites near the Twin Cities. Between then and 1940, his estate designs were built on the St. Croix River, Sunfish Lake, Gem

Lake, Turtle Lake, Christmas Lake, and White Bear Lake. After about 1940 his country estates were usually for clients living on Lake Minnetonka or outside of the immediate Twin Cities area near Winona, Owatonna, Red Wing, and St. James. He seemed particularly proud of the Daniels (see p. 44), Weyerhaeuser (see p. 66), Slade (see p. 60), Sweatt, and Gainey houses (see p. 52), for he singled them out in his 1954–55 first listing in *Who's Who in America*.[18]

Clearly the large country house was Lundie's forte. Beautiful, often irregular, sites and interested and tasteful clients with generous budgets allowed him to stipulate the complex forms, rich materials, and finely crafted details that he and his clients so enjoyed. Interior decoration, furniture design, and even garden design fell within his scope. He spent countless hours with his clients on the selection of interior finishes, details, and furnishings. If a desired item was not available through standard sources, he designed it for special fabrication by local craftsmen—in 1939 he even furnished a pattern for a hooked rug. Carl (Bud) Peterson of Edina was the contractor for many of his projects in the Twin Cities, and Joseph Pecore built several of the structures along the North Shore of Lake Superior.[19] In some cases it literally took years for the completion of a given project.

That Lundie was able to design throughout his career in this manner says as much about his clients as it does about him. Late in his life, he characterized his clients as representing an "aristocracy of good taste," and he was proud of the fact that he had third-generation clients from one of the same families which first had sought his services more than thirty years earlier.[20] After the 1930s Lundie was considered a fashionable residential architect, and there was a certain status attached to living in one of his houses. Indisputably there was genuine compatibility and respect between Lundie and his clients. Both sides desired a comfortable, historically reminiscent house that could be lived in easily and pleasurably, rather than a strongly innovative form or architectural presence that might make constant cerebral and emotional demands on the inhabitants.

After he became known as a specialist in residential design, he did only a few nonresidential projects. The 1946 designs for the chapel of Central Methodist Church in Winona and St. John's-in-the-Wilderness Church in White Bear Lake, both referring to Gothic prototypes, are the most important. Two of these non-residential projects were rare examples of modernism in his work. One was a monument commemorating the centennial of Father Lucien Galtier's construction of a log church in 1841 dedicated to St. Paul, an event that led to the naming of the city of St. Paul. An early study for it could best be described as Art Moderne, an outdated mode by 1941 but even so an unusual venture for Lundie. The final design was a simple, pink Minnesota granite boulder of irregular shape bearing two attached bronze plaques. The Merriam Park Community Center, built in St. Paul in 1951, was the second rare example of modern forms in Lundie's work, this time reflecting a simple, stripped-down cubic style that was current for utilitarian projects in the 1950s. It in no way manifested any personal imprint of Lundie. Vernacular rural architecture was the literal reference in his 1958 design for the red barn at the Gibbs Farm Museum in Lauderdale.

His major nonresidential work in later years was for the Minnesota Landscape Arboretum (see p. 98), a project dear to his heart. He designed, as a gift to the Arboretum, its entrance, pump house, trellis, and shelter, and he was at work on

Edwin Lundie, about 1940

Perspective rendering in pencil of a shelter at the Landscape Arboretum (1971)

its Educational and Research buildings at the time of his death. A cluster of simple, rectangular, gabled forms, it is not unlike his large, asymmetrical houses. Begun in 1971, it was completed by Bettenburg, Townsend, Stolte, and Comb.[21]

His insistence on good workmanship and his personal interest in antiques and interior decoration made Lundie the perfect architect for alterations that Mrs. Theodore Griggs had in mind for her 1862 forty-one-room limestone Italianate residence at 432 Summit Avenue in St. Paul. In the 1930s, with the advice of a friend, Mrs. Grenville Emmett, Mrs. Griggs bought whole rooms from French, English, and Italian seventeenth- and eighteenth-century houses, as well as countless pieces of furniture and works of art from the same periods. Lundie was called upon to reassemble and install all of it into a coherent, livable form. Hundreds of journal entries and drawings indicate the genuine interest he took in this work on the Griggs house. The result is a document of social history as well as a minor triumph of architectural eclecticism, for that kind of private wholesale importation of European rooms and art ended with World War II.

Mrs. Griggs also asked him to design a winter house in Florida, and beginning in 1936, she commissioned him to work on her country place on the Brule River in northwestern Wisconsin, a project that continued intermittently for twenty years. Artistry of a different, more rustic sort was required for the Brule River buildings, since they were built of local materials by local craftsmen.

The rusticity of the Brule River designs leads to consideration of some of Lundie's most personally expressive work—the seventeen cabins or summer houses he designed from 1940 to 1968 for sites along an eighty-mile stretch of the North Shore of Lake Superior. Lundie described his approach in a 1959 letter:

> All of the elements for an indigenous architecture were present. The bold scale of
> the rugged coast, the background of the forest, the intriguing beauty of the building

sites and then the great sweep of Lake Superior provided reason for a particular concept. Present were the materials, the lumber and timber from the surrounding forests, the stone from the hills. And present also were the skills of the artisan and craftsman to be explored, encouraged, and exploited.[22]

One of these deliberately remote and isolated retreats was begun in 1941 for his own family (see p. 88). Deeply responsive to nature since childhood, Lundie in later years enjoyed the increasingly extended sojourns at his cabin. In style and building technique, his own modestly scaled cabin is modeled on Norwegian country buildings. Local carpenters built with native pine, rough-sawn cedar, and North Shore stone. Lundie himself split shakes for its roof, carved its traditional corner posts, and made some of its furniture. He took pride in his skillful operation of a wood-turning lathe. Inside and out, the cabin exuded a cozy, personalized warmth.

On a vastly enlarged scale, Lutsen Resort (see p. 100) exemplifies the same rustic Scandinavian tradition. All of the other North Shore cabins have a similar aura of traditional design and craftsmanship, even though the specific ethnic or cultural references might differ from one project to another.

In carrying out these diverse projects, Lundie along the way became registered to practice architecture in Wisconsin, Iowa, and Florida, as well as in Minnesota where he had been registered since 1929.[23] As his practice and reputation grew, so did his professional standing, as evidenced by his advancement to Fellowship in the AIA. There were various other meritorious citations. Among them was a special award presented in 1957, his fiftieth year of practice, for high standards of professional practice from the Minnesota Society of Architects.[24]

Once his practice had stabilized, he became active in civic affairs. In 1937 he was named to the Planning Board of St. Paul and served continuously on it and its various committees for more than two decades, and in 1945 he was appointed to both the Redevelopment Commission and the Capitol Approach Commission. His association with the St. Paul Chapter of the Interprofessional Institute began in 1958.

Beginning about 1950 he was among a handful of local architects presciently aware of the desirability of preserving St. Paul's historic architecture that in the 1960s would be threatened with wholesale destruction in the name of urban renewal. He served on the Historic Sites Committee of the city planning board, which identified historically significant buildings and devised strategies for assisting in their preservation. Its work ultimately led to the publication in 1964 of *Historic St. Paul Buildings.*[25] He became active in various preservation matters through the local AIA Preservation Committee. In 1958 that committee success-fully negotiated a sympathetic remodeling of the St. Paul Public Library. Early on it proclaimed the architectural virtues of the Old Federal Courts Building, later renamed Landmark Center, a fine structure of the 1890s whose preserva-tion became a cause célèbre during the 1960s and 1970s.

Throughout his career, Lundie excelled as a perspective renderer. Like his houses, his drawings are meticulously executed. Unlike his houses, the drawings manifest consistent stylistic and formal evolution when studied in chronological sequence. His mature perspective renderings qualify as works of art quite apart from their significance as documentation.

Among Lundie's student drawings are a few sheets of architectural details, presumably done under the aegis of Atelier Masqueray. At the turn of the century, following the system of the École des Beaux-Arts, a large part of academic architectural education involved studying historic styles, particularly those of classical antiquity, and perfecting the skills of geometric drawing. With its precise unwavering line and carefully modulated tonal or value gradations, this kind of drawing is technically uniform and therefore anonymous in nature. It is difficult to detect personal graphic mannerisms in good geometric drawings. Either Lundie was not good at this kind of drawing, or—more likely, given his ultimate artistry as a perspective renderer—he simply did not like to do it.

Perspective rendering, that is the depiction of a building seen from an angle that displays two of its façades, usually in the context of its real or imaginary setting, is pictorial in nature. It derives from a topographical landscape pictorial tradition that can be traced back to the Renaissance desire to document, that is draw, ancient Roman buildings. It is essentially a subjective drawing that reveals the sometimes elusive character of a building as well as the specifics of its general appearance. Its successful artistic execution depends upon the intellectual comprehension of both abstract architectural form and two-dimensional pictorial form as well as mastery of drawing techniques. It was a presentation drawing whose main purpose was to persuade the client to build, unless occasionally it was an imaginary design intended only for publication. By the late nineteenth century, American architects considered a perspective rendering to be a layman's drawing and referred to it as a "show drawing."

Perspective rendering, unidentified ruins (1914)

Lundie's earliest known perspective renderings were the delicately executed 1913 Farm House Competition and a 1914 rendering of ruins. Both are tentative in execution but exhibit a promising freehand touch. A more densely rendered perspective of a castle, dated 1916, depicts architectural forms with closely hatched or cross-hatched soft pencil lines. The full tonal range suggests the visual appearance of black-and-white photographs, and Lundie probably was working from a photograph in an exercise designed both to further his acquaintance with historic architecture and to advance his rendering techniques. Drawing from photographs was a common procedure, and Lundie did it from time to time throughout his career.

Beginning from an artistically unpromising state in the mid-nineteenth century, when the harsh, angular, insensitive lines of perspective renderings resembled commercial wood engravings, American renderers, or delineators as they also were called, by the early 1880s had developed a recognizable style of rendering based on a beautiful freehand linear technique. Holyoke and Masqueray were undistinguished perspective renderers, but Cass Gilbert was one of the best. Gilbert's freehand student drawings and sketches, a few of which were published during the late 1870s and early 1880s in *American Architect and Building News*, were among the drawings that Lundie studied during his lunch hours in the Holyoke office. Typically they were delicately rendered Ruskinian vignettes that merely suggested form, detail, and surfaces.

Watercolor accents on one of Lundie's earliest office renderings, a 1919 pencil study for St. Rita's Academy, recall Gilbert's work. One of his first pen-and-ink renderings, a perspective of the Sioux Falls Cathedral, also dates from 1919. Although still somewhat tentative technically, like his student perspectives, there are a few visually emphatic peripheral details, such as the foliage in the lower left corner.

Pen-and-ink drawings done between 1919 and 1921 show a growing formal and technical competence. Groups of longer, sensitive lines with occasional strong black focal points are coherently organized compositionally, and peripheral details such as sky and landscape are beautifully executed.

Among the many renderers whose work Lundie clipped out of architectural magazines, two stand out as being particularly important in the formation of his own mature style: Harvey Ellis and Bertram Grosvenor Goodhue. Although Ellis, one of the most influential American renderers whose work was published during the 1880s and 1890s, died three years before Lundie entered the world of architecture, his beautiful drawings were republished in several architectural magazines between 1908 and 1912, Lundie's student years.[26] In the work of both Ellis and Lundie, there is a similar control, variation, and flourish of freehand line that is particularly apparent in foliage and other accessory details. Lundie built up sharper and more sudden contrasts of light and dark, however, and occasionally even used solidly filled black areas, a Goodhue mannerism. There was in fact a similarity between Lundie's Sioux Falls projects and Goodhue's romanticizing Gothic work both in architectural and rendering style. Gilbert, Ellis, and Goodhue thus seem to have been the major influences that guided Lundie as he perfected his own rendering style.

Lundie's mature artistry as a perspective renderer received recognition, even enabling him to earn a living as a free-lance draftsman or delineator at several stages in his career. In 1925 his renderings were included in an AIA exhibition in New York, and in the same year eight of them were featured in *Architectural Record*.[27] Occasionally his drawings were exhibited in various Twin Cities locations.

After Lundie began independent practice in 1919, he mainly did pencil renderings. A 1922 pen-and-ink rendering of a house (see p. 26) may be one of his last in that medium. The house is overshadowed by the baroque graphic treatment of peripheral, contextual details.

As another 1922 drawing indicates, he found pencil to be an equally sympathetic medium. His technique involved first laying out a framework of light straight-edge lines. Then different pencils of varying degrees of hardness and sharpness were used to produce lines of great delicacy and lightness, of moderate width and medium value, and of thick, black intensity. The range is from broken, crinkled delicate lines, made with a pencil sharpened on sandpaper, to solidly stroked black areas occasionally enhanced with gray wash. One senses the rhythm of the hand as it rapidly drew the closely hatched, fan-shaped areas of different tonalities. Individual passages in the drawings are a visual delight, and it is beautifully realized as an artistic whole. Lundie had by now reached a point of true artistry as a delineator, and throughout the next three decades he did dozens of beautiful perspective renderings.

By 1935 a denser, darker overall effect began to appear. He used softer, blunter pencils, and general tonal harmonies were more important artistically than individual linear elements. After 1939 he achieved effects of flickering light and cast shadows by a system of hundreds of short segments of line that thickly filled the entire drawing. By 1940 the size of many of the drawings began to decrease, and

Perspective rendering in pencil of a residence (1922)

a particularly touching 1958 drawing of a house measures only three by four inches. On a vastly reduced scale it contains many of the artistic elements of the earlier, larger drawings. The last dated perspective drawing in Lundie's papers, done in 1962 when he was seventy-six, was of the Minnesota Landscape Arboretum Pavilion. The bravura display of sheer technique noted in the earlier renderings is gone, but a quiet artistry remains.

As Lundie entered his seventh decade he gradually began to withdraw from extracurricular professional and civic commitments, although he occasionally in the 1960s continued to jury the registration examination drawings for the Mid-Central State Conference of the National Council of Architectural Registrations Boards. Beginning about 1960, he curtailed his practice. After his wife of forty-one years died in 1968, he moved from his house in Mahtomedi to the St. Paul Athletic Club. In 1971 when his health had seriously deteriorated, he ceased work completely and moved to Fargo, North Dakota, in order to be near his daughter, but he retained his office in the Endicott Building until the end of his life. After a brief period of hospitalization in Fargo, Edwin Lundie died on January 8, 1972. His funeral was at the church of St. John-in-the-Wilderness in White Bear Lake, which he had designed, and he was buried in Roselawn Cemetery in suburban St. Paul.

Lundie typified a kind of architect who was the norm in the United States throughout the nineteenth century and even into the first two decades of the twentieth but who disappeared from the profession more than half a century ago. He was fundamentally self-taught, learned outside of an academic program, began as an apprentice, advanced to draftsman, and after many years obtained independent professional status. For this type of preparation alone, Lundie's career is of interest. In addition many of his designs and almost all of his mature perspective renderings constitute achievements of merit that rightfully should be incorporated into the multifaceted story of twentieth-century American architecture.

Lundie in 1969

Lundie articulated the necessity of mastering the generic formal elements of mass, scale, and proportion, along with a knowledge of and response to the unique qualities of each building material and craft.[28] To a degree these things can be learned, but truly effective use of them depends upon an innate artistic sensibility, and this quality Lundie possessed without a doubt.

Lundie perhaps offered the best summation of his career in a remark that he made to his daughter during his last year: "I have had a wonderful life. I have done just what I wanted to do."[29] One indeed senses exactly this quality of pleasure and satisfaction in his distinctive architecture and in his beautiful perspective renderings.

NOTES

As architectural curator of the Minnesota Museum of Art, I supervised the transfer of perspective renderings, construction documents, office records (except for the financial ledger that, by family decision, was destroyed), clippings files, books, and personal journals from Lundie's office in the Endicott Building to the Minnesota Museum of Art shortly after Lundie died. In

Perspective rendering in pencil of residences (ca. 1939)

1982 the Lundie archives were transferred from the museum to the Northwest Architectural Archives at the University of Minnesota. Now known as the Edwin Lundie Papers, they have been accessioned, cataloged, and indexed. I thank Alan Lathrop, curator of the archives, and Barbara Bezat, assistant to the curator, for their help as I recently reviewed this material.

Following the transfer of the Lundie material to the museum, I read the yearly journals that Lundie kept more or less continuously for much of his adult life, perused the drawings and other materials, and pieced together a detailed personal and professional account of Lundie and his work, which was summarized in Eileen Michels, *Encounter with Artists Number Nine: Edwin Hugh Lundie (1886–1972)* (St. Paul: Minnesota Museum of Art, 1972), the catalog to accompany the exhibition I organized of Lundie's work shown at the museum November 16, 1972–January 7, 1973. This essay is based on that work.

1. Samuel Lundie was born in New York, and Emma Hitchcock Lundie in Ohio. Samuel Lundie died in 1916 and Emma Lenore Lundie in 1944. Ellen Lundie Thompson to author, May 8, 1972.
2. Thompson to author, May 8, 1972. Records of the Cedar Rapids schools for the 1870s are not available; phone call to author November 3, 1993. A secretary in the office of the Salem public schools found a record book from 1903 listing Edwin Lundie as attending Salem High School in 1903. It gave his age as sixteen. No other information about Lundie or his family was recorded in it; memo from Jan Ecklein to author, November 5, 1994.
3. Lundie recalled that he arrived in St. Paul in 1904; "Edwin H. Lundie FAIA," *Northwest Architect,* May–June 1969, p. 19.
4. Thompson to author, May 8, 1972.
5. Lundie spoke of his association with Gilbert in a paper, "I Knew Cass Gilbert," at the annual meeting of the Society of Architectural Historians, Minneapolis, January 28, 1961, copy in Lundie Papers. Coincidentally, I presented a paper on another architect at that same meeting, and I remember Lundie as rather slight in frame, white haired, and nattily attired in a brown tweed suit. For more on Gilbert, see Robert A. Jones, "Cass Gilbert: Forgotten Giant," *Northwest Architect,* Nov.–Dec. 1959, p. 28–30, 31, 51–52; Patricia Anne Murphy, "The Early Career of Cass Gilbert, 1878 to 1895" (master's thesis, University of Virginia, 1979).
6. Alan K. Lathrop, "A French Architect in Minnesota: Emmanuel L. Masqueray, 1861–1917," *Minnesota History* 47 (Summer 1980): 42–56. Henry F. Withey and Elsie Rathburn Withey, *Biographical Dictionary of American Architects (Deceased)* (Los Angeles: New Age Pub. Co., 1956), states, "Mr. Masqueray should also be remembered as one of the founders of the first Beaux-Arts Atliers [*sic*] established in New York. Largely due to his efforts the academic training of the Paris Beaux-Arts was made attainable to American students" (397–98).
7. The other founders were Frank Abrahamson, Beaver Wade Day, Magnus Jemne, Hiram Livingston, Fred Slifer, Frank Smalley, and Herbert Sullwold. The "Membership Roster and History Brochure, Gargoyle Club of St. Paul, 1960," with an introduction by Robert H. Kerr, president, is an account of the early history and financial record of the Gargoyle Club; copy in Minnesota Historical Society. Between 1917 and 1921 the Gargoyle Club owned the German Presbyterian Church, a delightfully picturesque 1890 design from the office of Gilbert and Taylor. Cass Gilbert, Charles Maginnis, and Ralph Adams Cram were notable architects who gave talks to the members of the Gargoyle Club. I am indebted to Dale Mulfinger for pointing out that the Gargoyle Club still exists.
8. "In Conversation with Mr. Lundie," 105 (below).
9. Lathrop, "A French Architect," 56, refers to ten unfinished commissions; however, the agreement with the three architects and the Merchants Trust and Savings Bank, the estate administrators, refers to thirteen.
10. Thompson to author, May 8, 1972.
11. "Edwin Lundie FAIA," 19; Lundie mistakenly recalls 1917.

12. Susan Barker, "Keepers of the Flame," *Minneapolis/St. Paul,* Jan. 1990, p. 103–5, 124–25, describes the renovation of the Lundie house by its new owners.

13. Lundie served as chapter president, 1927–28 and 1932–33, secretary-treasurer, 1923–24, and vice-president, 1927–28. He served on the Executive Committee, 1928–29, 1931, 1932–38, 1940–48, and as chairman of the Credentials Committee, 1949–52. Beginning in the 1940s he occasionally also attended the annual national conventions of the AIA.

14. The following people worked for him through the years: Clayton Avison, Stanley Twitchell, Ralph Smalley, Russell England, William Burgstadt, Herman Wenke, Herman Walters, Frank Clark, Arthur Cayon, Peter Linhoff, William Napier, Francis Gorman, James Richards, Louis Bramstedt and two people referred to only by their last names, Alban and Molitor. An accountant was occasionally hired for bookkeeping. At various times Lundie seemed to depend on Avison, Smalley, England, Burgstadt, Bramstedt, and Clark more than the others. Some of his employees were students from the St. Paul vocational school.

15. *St. Paul Dispatch,* May 14, 1969, p. 25.

16. *Journal of American Institute of Architects* 10 (July 1948): 27.

17. *House and Garden,* May 1940, p. 26–27, June 1948, p. 98 (his own cabin), Feb. 1960, p. 57 (Sweatt house), Mar. 1960, p. 108–11 (Sweatt house).

18. *Who's Who in America* (Chicago: Marquis Who's Who, 1954–55), 29:1592.

19. Lundie's surviving papers rarely mention contractors. I am indebted to Dale Mulfinger for this information.

20. "In Conversation," 106 (below).

21. David Gebhard and Tom Martinson, *A Guide to the Architecture of Minnesota* (Minneapolis: University of Minnesota Press, 1977), 117.

22. *Cook County News Herald,* Feb. 10, 1959.

23. "Edwin H. Lundie FAIA," 19, again is inaccurate.

24. *Northwest Architect,* July–Aug. 1957, p. 34–37, published the citation along with a program honoring Lundie based upon *This Is Your Life,* a television program popular at the time. The citation reads:

    Edwin H. Lundie. For fifty years an architect. For fifty years a sensitive designer inspired by the love of creating beauty. For fifty years a friend and sympathetic counsellor to countless clients whose gratitude continually deepens as they discover new delights in already familiar buildings. His work embodies the gentle thoughtfulness of the man. For fifty years a beloved colleague. By his example the future of the profession glows more brightly. May he show us the way for years to come.

25. *Historic St. Paul Buildings* (St. Paul: Planning Board of St. Paul, 1964), with text by H. F. Koeper.

26. *Architectural Review* 15, no. 12 (Dec. 1908).

27. *Architectural Record* 57 (June 1925): 533–48.

28. "In Conversation," 107 (below).

29. Thompson to author, May 8, 1972.

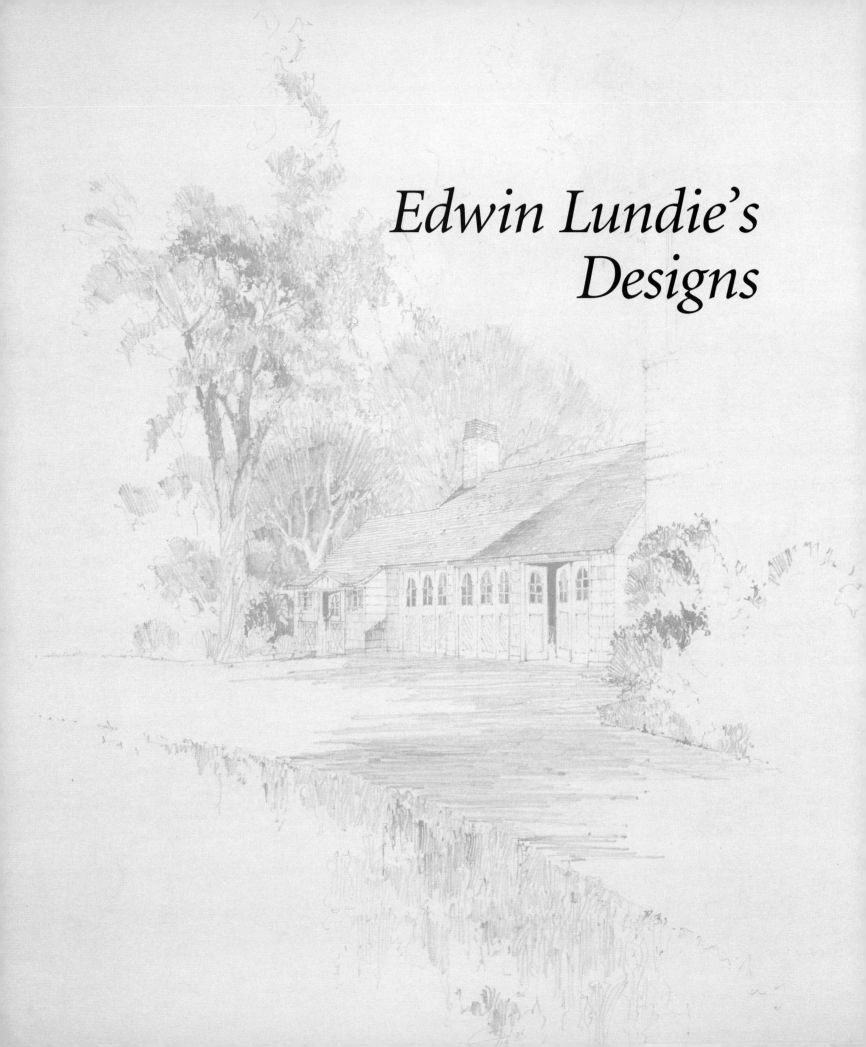

Edwin Lundie's Designs

Edwin Lundie's Designs

DALE MULFINGER

For roughly fifty years Edwin Lundie practiced architecture in Minnesota under his own name. Working for a clientele that he categorized as the "aristocracy of good taste," Lundie honed his design ideas over the course of some three hundred projects.[1] Yet from the time of one of his earliest houses, the Stakman house (see p. 80), until his final project of the Landscape Arboretum (see p. 98), there is a consistency in the ideas that form the underpinnings of his structures. His interest in simple, vernacular forms, evident in the Stakman design, was retained throughout his career. Whether gleaning his references from New England, the French countryside, rural England, or agrarian Scandinavia, he consistently drew from the vernacular forms that connected him to his clients' tastes.

Lundie acknowledged that Cass Gilbert's influence "shaped my attitude and my entire outlook toward my work."[2] Interestingly, however, whereas Lundie adopted the common Beaux-Arts model of quoting a design's source, he apparently rejected Gilbert's Beaux-Arts images and search for grand projects. Rather, Lundie appeared to prefer the small, modest, and intimate. Indeed, his larger houses are an assemblage of small structures, and his doorways so low that even he might have stooped to go through them. Lundie exhibited a humility in his work, showing greater concern for detail, scale, proportion, and craftsmanship than for Beaux-Arts grandeur.

Lundie's reasons for focusing on these particular designs is open to speculation. Possibly his humble upbringing propelled him not to fame but rather to service, as in a job well done, for Lundie certainly excelled in the craft of making a house and detailing its parts. He appeared comfortable with the scope and scale of residential projects and was content to live in his own modest house, which he remodeled, for more than fifty years.

Lundie's drawing for the remodeling of his own house (1922)

Lundie's remodeled house, showing his touches in the shutters and doorway

As his career evolved through a steady stream of residential commissions, his execution through detail became the particular signature in his work. He never stopped drawing, producing designs for floor patterns, hardware, light fixtures, moldings, and carved ornament. Carpenters noted that pieces of his cabins went together like those of a fine piece of furniture, and it is in this area that his work achieved special recognition.

His imagination was fueled at an early age, as he noted later in life:

I think I attribute my enjoyment in this profession to the fact that my grandparents and my parents fed me all of the romantic fiction of that age which was good. It was a high order of thing, it was very imaginative, I think sometimes to the point of exaggeration and I think that's been true with me in my architecture. You can always land with a dull thud if you have gotten up there in the clouds too far. I think mastery of line and mass and scale and proportion is important; it is part of the working tools. Knowledge of the materials and crafts you're working is infinitely important. We're talking about design detail now and there are certain attributes of materials that call for different treatments, of doing things much finer, on a finer scale with some than with others.[3]

Lundie observed his fellow architects shifting their ideas away from the quotations of historical precedents and into the search for innovative ideas in the pursuit of new social agendas. Concerns for housing a growing population and the industrialization of house construction, although never a total reality, significantly influenced his colleagues. Lundie likely would have agreed with Joseph Hudnet, dean of the Harvard Graduate School of Design, who wrote in 1945 that

> the factory-built house, as I imagine it, fails to furnish my mind with that totality of impression with which the word house (meaning building occupied by a family) has always filled it: it leaves unexhibited that idea of home about which there cling so many nuances of thought and sentiment. My readers may count me a romanticist if they wish—and perhaps they can conceive of a home without romance?—but I do not discover in any one of these types of house prefigured in the published essays of technologists that promise of happiness which, in houses, is the important quality of all appearances. . . . My impression is obviously shared by a wide public—circumstance which explains in part the persistence with which people, however, enamored of science, cling to the familiar patterns of their houses.[4]

Lundie indeed clung to familiar patterns of houses and devoted his scientific energy to the technologies of the craftsman, a whole cadre of which he began to nurture. To an interviewer, he stated, "I have nothing against progress but I become concerned about the quality of it."[5]

Lundie designed the Stakman house (see p. 80) through a process of envisioning massing, plan, construction, and site as one harmonious beginning and used the process of the *esquisse* or rough sketch to bring the totality of the house into focus.[6] For the Stakman house, Lundie assembled simple gable shapes in a visually congenial asymmetrical ensemble. He utilized the mass to cluster around the entry, forming a courtyardlike spatial enclosure. The entry door is clearly marked by the columnar molding and arched pediment set slightly and casually to the side of the primary façade. The door opens onto a center hall and stairway, which organizes the plan. Both the dining room and living room have three exterior walls, their windows offering both light and ventilation. A series of built-in cabinets embellish the rooms—corner cabinets in the dining room, bookshelves in the library, and a mantel over the living-room fireplace. French doors open onto a well-exposed porch, which presents its gable face to the street. Set diagonally to the street on a hillside and parallel to the alley, this modest structure is a picturesque image of Hudnet's "promise of happiness."

Lundie was said by his staff to have begun his designs through a process of research and reconnaissance in his library. After meeting with clients and visiting the site, Lundie would ensconce himself in one of the better libraries known to local architects—his own. His library included journals of both professional and lay interest, monographs (including European and New England tour books of etchings and photographs by the noted etcher Samuel Chamberlain[7] and others), scrapbooks wherein he had assembled product information and society news (along with notes on details), and the usual technical manuals common to an architectural office. Here he immersed himself in the vocabulary of possibilities through which to engage the *esquisse*. This process was not necessarily a quick one, and the effort could take several days. He would eventually settle at his drafting desk with *esquisse* in hand to test and develop his initial hypothesis through a series of drafts. Plans, sections, elevations, and an accurate perspective would emerge, ready to be presented to his client.[8]

His first attempt did not always meet his expectations or gain his client's endorsement. On at least one occasion, the Weed house, he created as many as eleven different schemes, each drafted in a complete presentation. Sometimes he developed beautiful and elaborate pencil exterior perspectives, showing the settings with foliage, or interior perspectives, noting not only the cabinet and trim details but also furniture to provide scale for the room. After a client accepted a scheme, Lundie completed each house design through an elaborate set of drawings for construction. To this set he added a modest list of specifications, calling for particular wood finishes or a selection of standard hardware. After construction began, he executed template drawings with full-scale details to aid construction crews and fabrication craftsmen. He made site visits as necessary to interpret his work to the builders.

This consistency of process and intent was exhibited throughout his work and in his final project, the Minnesota Landscape Arboretum. Of its design he said:

> Wait until you will see the total building out there. A lot of people were a little amazed when they saw the size of the beams on the ground, but when they're up and in place, they take on an entirely different dimension. It's a scale and the line of the whole building that's the thing. All of this has been a great pleasure for me—to be associated with something that is all building up and not tearing down. We didn't destroy anything out there. I don't think we've cut down a tree yet.[9]

A structure substantially larger than the Stakman house, the Arboretum nevertheless contains some similar design themes. Like the house, it pulls the wings of the building around an entry space or courtyard. Additive gabled building elements project individual rooms as "wings of light."[10] Each room has its own order, usually symmetrical. Although the Arboretum certainly has Norman or English precedents, it does not draw heavily from a specific source. Its source is just as likely the vernacular barns of the Midwest.[11] Its detailing evolved through the many transformations Lundie pursued on numerous projects with his favorite craftsmen. The turned, wooden light fixtures, the column brackets, the lamppost bracket and lantern, the obelisklike post tops,[12] the wooden cartouche over the rear windows,[13] the brick detailing on the wall of the dining terrace, the specific character of the timber-framed shelter, and the exquisite detail of the pump house—these are recognizable Lundie details. Although this design was rendered large for a substantial program, it retains a humility of expression, a picturesque quality that engages the architecture with its site.[14] Through the process of the *esquisse* Lundie exhibited the "promise of happiness" in all his work, from institutions to residences.

Throughout the *esquisse* process Lundie drew reference to the whole of the house in one simultaneous beginning, which connected his work to the entirety of his collected references. These references recalled a way of life for his clients. Educated for the most part in eastern schools or with teachers educated in the East, Lundie and his clients probably recognized Europe and New England as being the sources of cultural identity. Although Lundie himself had not traveled, he vicariously visited foreign locales through the romantic images housed in his library, which became an extension of the stories told by his grandparents. His

*In succeeding drawings
Lundie showed
a reworking of the design
for the dining room addition
to the Daniels house.*

The Robinson cabin under construction

images were like the setting of a story, rendered real in the glens of rolling mid-western countryside or along a city street in St. Paul. Like stories, they built from a central theme and developed through the rich detail of each character.

The primary attributes of each of his houses as embodied in the *esquisse* were: 1. the arrival experience, 2. the massing of forms, 3. the order of rooms, 4. the stairway, 5. the location of chimneys, 6. the relation of rooms to sources of light, and 7. specific site concerns. All of these elements embodied his identifiable style. His penchant for simple gable forms may have been as much to simplify the formula necessary to reach a conclusion as it was a reference to the vernacular forms of his region. Relying upon known types or solutions aided him as the designer moving through the complex process of synthesizing diverse programmatic, site, and budget constraints and parameters.[15] Such methods, in vogue during the years of his apprenticeship, fell into disfavor with architects in post–World War II America. By the 1970s architects were reconsidering this process as a means of connecting to the public discourse on design.[16]

Lundie employed the *esquisse* method in all his projects, large and small. In small projects, such as his own cabin on the North Shore of Lake Superior (see p. 88) or the Spink house in St. Paul (see p. 79), in one primary gable he resolved all of the competing programmatic and site forces while still giving the building stylistic or typologic reference. The Spink house emulated simple Cape Cod images while his cabin derived from Scandinavian stavra.[17] In the Spink house he added a gable for the garage, which is parallel to and attached to the house.

Larger programs led to larger ensembles of gabled units in a variety of configurations. The Little house near Winona (see p. 54) is a linear grouping of parallel units, with the living room unit being the largest and thrusting out into

The Searles and Biester/Phelps houses

the site like a gigantic bay window. His later addition of another bedroom unit at the north end of the house seems as if it always belonged. The Fiterman house (see p. 74) wraps gabled units around an outdoor courtyard, organizing the plan as if the courtyard were yet another room and rendering this large house small and discrete. The Driscoll house (see p. 48) adds an angular wing to an early Lundie design and completes the ensemble with a mass at the end that seems to be a little house itself. The large ensembles often used principal rooms to serve both as functional space and for circulation. The Daniels house (see p. 44) living room provides access to the couple's realm beyond.[18] Similarly, as in most hunting lodges, the great room of the Thompson Shooting Box (see p. 64) separates the diverse sleeping accommodations.

Many of Lundie's plans spread forms out so that major rooms could receive light on parallel sides. Yet he often designed compact schemes that necessitated rooms in corners and thus had incoming light on perpendicular and adjacent sides. Such schemes were common in Colonial houses where the entry was in the center of the façade and an integral part of the central-hall plan. In the neighboring Colonial-style Searles, Schmitz, and Biester/Phelps houses, the plans exhibit subtle differences. The Searles house has a chimney at each end, the Schmitz a chimney at one end, and the Biester/Phelps house a chimney in the center. This combination—center hall, center chimney—is also a feature of the modest Anderson and Spink houses. In the larger, Colonial-style Voss and Delander houses, the center hall opens up for a grand staircase.

Lundie often placed the front entry, a central component of Colonial plans, at the corner and made it a less prominent feature. In such schemes the massing of the house suggested a simple entry rather than a hierarchy of the façade. The Cotswold style of the Aberle and Binswanger houses features a corner entry articulated with special stone features and details. Although the precedent for a house in Sunfish Lake was a center-hall Cape Cod, the larger plan necessitated a corner entry, converting the traditional Cape Cod entry into a connection between the terrace and the yard.

In small structures, such as cabins, entries often opened directly into primary rooms and thus were placed on the cabin's lake side. Some cabins, such as the Robinson and McDonald cabins, have covered entry canopies on the land side. The Stocke cabin includes an arcaded entry within a secondary gable. Entries were often the focus of courtyards, as can be seen in the Stakman, Sweatt, Gainey, Winters, and Rerat houses. The Rerat house courtyard has an external stairway to the entry door. The Stocke house in Rochester has one of the more unusual entries; it is attached to an outer corner of the mass.

Chimneys, in addition to conveying smoke out of the house and connecting the fireplace to the formal room arrangements, have also been elements of sheer delight in Lundie's detailing. At times they are integral elements of stone end walls, such as those in the Weed house, and often they are central anchors of the primary gable, such as the ones in the Sunfish Lake house. His chimneys can also be lyrical and fanciful. The Aberle and Daniels houses have twisted chimneys that look as if the mason had employed a whirlwind. The Weyerhaeuser guest

The front hall of the Voss house

The reworked design for the corner entry of a Cape Cod house

The front entry of the Winters house

cabin has a chimney topped with its own cabinlike structure. The Shields and Daniels houses have majestic grouped chimneys modeled on the English tradition of fine brick work.[19] Chimneys and fireplaces were often set into corners, such as at the Arboretum and the Olson cabin. In Lundie's cabin the fireplace has a major presence both in giving the room character and in subdividing it into functional zones. In the majestic, timber-framed space of the Robinson cabin, the chimney graces the interior with its Flemish detailed brickwork, called muisetanden (mouse teeth) coping.[20] A similar detail appears on the Aberle house exterior but in this case rendered in slate.

With chimneys come fireplaces, and many of Lundie's are quite elaborate. Like his houses, some large, others small, fireplaces are at times modest, discrete, and simply charming and at other times grand and magnificent. In the Rerat house a quaint, tiled fireplace graces the kitchen, as does a more rustic one in the Merritt house. A magnificent hearth adorns the rathskeller in the Gainey house. The Slade country house has fireplaces in both scales, a large one in the main hall and more intimate and rustic ones in bedrooms next to window seats. The connection of fireplace to window seat is also important in the lakeside Stocke

The chimney of the Weyerhaeuser guest cabin

The Shields house chimney

The living-room fireplace of the Sweatt house

cabin. The window seat is large enough to curl up on and take a nap or to recline on and warm your toes at the hearth while listening to waves lapping on the shore. In many of the refined, Colonial-style city houses, fireplaces have elaborate wood moldings, none finer than that found in the couple's bedroom of the Fiterman house or in the dining room at the Weyerhaeuser house. In Lundie's house in Mahtomedi, remodeling included a modest fireplace in his bedroom, complete with a tiny storage compartment for his pipe.

Finely detailed trim, molding, paneled walls, and storage spaces were common features in many of his houses. He often used storage elements to aid in the division of space and thus placed them in interior walls. His addition to the Ellsinger country house has thick bedroom walls because they incorporate storage areas and closets. Ceilings are dropped in the bedroom entryways to enhance the perception of storage-in-the-walls. In the Merritt house the same can be said of the passage between the living room and the den where both interior-wall storage and a lowered ceiling are used to move these rooms farther apart. Storage was also added to exterior walls, occasionally giving the impression of windows residing in thick walls, such as in the den and bedroom of the Fiterman house or in the bedrooms of the Thompson Shooting Box.

Lundie's window selections formed sensitive resolutions to the differences between interior and exterior criteria. By present-day standards his interiors seem dark, although this perception is due in part to the dark hues of wood, paint, and fabrics and often dense drapery that prevailed in the 1930s and 1940s. He appears to have had a penchant for tall, slender windows or French doors in main-floor social spaces. He divided the sash into multiple lights and frequently used triple-hung windows in main-floor rooms. The Weed house may be unique

The fireplace in Lundie's house

The Weed house showing the gable roof and the bay

in its use of triple-hung windows on both levels of the house. Bay windows were common in many spaces, notably dining rooms, and were often capped with flat roofs for no ascertainable reason. A particularly awkward example of this type of roof is in the Weed house where a gable roof element interrupts the main roof but does not extend over the bay projection. Equally prevalent among Lundie designs was the use of the bow window, such as in the living rooms of the Fiterman and Gainey houses.

In cabin designs his windows were usually hinged casements that swung outward to catch the summer breezes. Some cabins have large picture windows unbroken by muntin bars, an appearance that seems at odds with the detail found in other elements. Cabin roofs are broken by both shed and gable dormers, letting light into rooms at the rooftop level. The Robinson cabin is an excellent example of shed dormers, as is the Olson cabin for gable dormers. Several cabins and houses have been remodeled to admit more light or to allow residents a greater view of the lake water beyond, but rarely have these changes been successful visually.

Lundie's designs for attic windows embodied the dreams arising from the stories of his grandparents. No window has a more poignant impact than the one in the attic of the Sweatt house, which is perched on one of the finest points on

Lake Minnetonka. As you recline on a bed with your head comfortably resting on a pillow, your view of this magnificent lake is tightly framed by a one-foot-square window. This might be referred to as a Zen view.[21]

Divided light muntins in windows were generally of common scale, although some have unique wood profiles. In the Gainey house the back porch window has an outer screen that has the appearance of mammoth muntins subdividing the window. The Daniels house has leaded, diamond-shape lights, similar to those found in English houses. In the Sweatt house small, round porthole-like windows add what could be called a New England coastal character. Lundie's own house, as well as other Lundie-designed houses, featured bottle glass in transoms. Some of the most beautiful windows, framed in timber with hand-chamfered edges, are in the Stocke house in Rochester. Oriel windows, a type of bay window, adorn the public façade of the Aberle house.

Dormers, an element Lundie used in many cabins, embellished both city and country houses. For informally composed, picturesque façades, Lundie varied dormer sizes to form compositions with gable ends, most notably on the Daniels entry façade. Dormers on the Aberle house appear quite whimsical, as the function of at least one of them is certainly suspect as it is too small to have any utility. A familiar trait of Lundie's dormers is the application of diagonal siding, paralleling the roof slope. This pattern was characteristic of residences in the southern colonies of early America, especially in such places as Chapel Hill, North Carolina, or Williamsburg. It is a rare occurrence in Minnesota and frequently a sign that the design is by Lundie.

Real movable shutters, often attached to windows, provide storm protection and winter warmth, but Lundie probably included them for aesthetic purposes. The wood slats of several of the shutters have cut-out shapes. Of particular note are the leaf patterns, like falling leaves across the board. Several houses in the University Grove area of St. Paul have a variety of shutter designs. The catch used to hold the shutters open also came under Lundie's purview.

Like windows, doors also exhibit Lundie's attention to detail. Notable is the scale of his main entry doors. Whereas standard entry doors are three feet wide by six feet, eight inches tall, his door designs were often three feet, eight inches wide by six feet, three inches tall. This combination of lower and broader dimensions significantly changed the scale of the door and altered the experience of entering the house. Entering can be seen as an act of humility, as a guest is honored to be invited into the private world of a family. How Lundie evolved this scale is unknown, but such doors appear in the beautiful drawings of artist Carl Larsson's books.[22]

Dutch doors, split horizontally into halves, were also a popular door design of Lundie's. The Z frame necessary to keep the door from rocking was emphasized as a door detail in both single- and double-Z patterns. Doors in steeply gabled, second-floor rooms where the ceiling formed an acute angle with the wall often had round tops. A few large doors, such as the entry door at Lutsen, had a two-square motif. A similar motif appeared on the doors of some furniture that Lundie designed.

Door hardware seems to have been of particular interest to Lundie. He developed exquisite wood latches on many doors, notably those in the second-floor rooms in the Sunfish Lake house. But he also worked in metal, creating both

The screen wall of the porch of the Gainey house

The Sweatt house porthole-style windows

Lundie executed a double-door design for a Sunfish Lake house.

The main entry door of the Shields house

Lundie designed round-top doors to fit in the second-floor hallway of the Sunfish Lake house.

door latches and hinges. Nowhere is this penchant more elaborately expressed than in the Slade country house and the Weyerhaeuser cabin. Each room displays a different wild game theme, such as pheasant, deer, or trout, on the door hinges. Latches, although not exhibiting figurative motifs, also varied from room to room. One can only surmise the joy of Lundie, the designer, as he sketched another full-scale, template drawing of fish, fowl, or wild beast. Like characters in his grandparents' stories, these animals spring to life with each creaking swing of the door.

The exterior façades of Lundie structures were usually wood, either horizontal lap siding or vertical board and batten. In his cabins, some residences, Lutsen Resort, and the Arboretum, he used several differently patterned wood surfaces, each framed with broad boards. Lundie used this technique to break up broad expanses of façade and identify the structure as timber frame. Although the timber frame itself is shielded from the destructive force of the weather, these framed segments give reference to the timber structure inside. Lundie also used brick and stone for exteriors, but stucco, a frequently used surface material, is seldom found in his work.

Of particular interest to Lundie was the use of timber frame, post, beam, truss, and perlin systems both in his own cabin and in almost all of his work on the North Shore of Lake Superior.[23] This interest may have been nurtured by the lodge quality of some of the living rooms of his early buildings, such as the Daniels house, or it could have surfaced as he worked on the ecclesiastical projects of his mentors, Gilbert and Masqueray. Cass Gilbert designed some beautiful, timber-roofed churches, such as St. Stephens in St. Paul, in which Lundie had a minor part. Beginning with the Slade country house and following with his own cabin, he began to explore a more complete expression of timber-frame construction. Where he happened upon the Scandinavian stavra may never be known, although it is possible that some of the Scandinavian craftsmen constructing the Slade project knew of this form of construction. Heresay has it that he gained his knowledge of this technique from a copy of *National Geographic*. Little information on the subject was in print at the time he began both his and the Daniels cabins in 1941. He had worked on the Thompson Shooting Box the previous year, developing a rather nautical-looking truss for the main hall. But his own cabin marks the beginning of designing a complete building fashioned like a piece of furniture. With a place for everything and everything in its place, these structures have a tight constructive logic that may supplant the picturesque quality that otherwise generated his work.

Because materials and labor were scarce or unavailable during World War II, Lundie did not return to the Scandinavian timber frame until the Kromschroeder commission in 1945. By then he had had time to idealize this type and to have spent a few summers in his own cabin. The Kromschroeder cabin (see p. 85) appears to epitomize the concept of cabin building as furniture building. The order of elements is precise and complete. Oversized, lathe-turned corner columns articulate the corners that rest on crossed sill plates, which themselves decoratively protrude beyond their intersection. Six-inch-square vertical posts divide the façade into equal units, some filled with windows, some with doors, and some solid. A six-by-ten-inch top plate is doweled to each post. Longitudinal eight-by-ten-inch girders hold the gallery (attic). They bear on the gabled end walls, piercing the wall, and have a large key inserted to stabilize the end wall. Six-inch-square beams rest on the girders, tying across the gable roof to counteract the outward force of the roof. In but a few simple drawings the whole of this modest twenty-by-twenty-four-foot cabin is laid forth for fabrication and assembly.

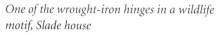

A wood latch for an interior door, Slade house

In the postwar period, Lundie designed several cabins in this genre, but only one as modest in scale as the Kromschroeder cabin. As sites along Lake Superior became more accessible due to improved highways, the scale of investment in lake homes increased, resulting in both larger structures and multiple-building complexes. In his final days as a functioning architect, he was still working on both the Arboretum and the Weyerhaeuser cabin. Absent from the Weyerhaeuser cabin (see p. 94) is any specific reference to Scandinavian themes; rather an elegant timber-frame construct that is uniquely Lundie emerged. The façade still referenced the segmented nature of the frame inside. The timber-frame, diagonal structure of the screened porch at the guest cabin showed further experimentation. The logs of the end walls give a decorative element to the gable end of the guest cabin.

One of the wrought-iron hinges in a wildlife motif, Slade house

Lundie's cabin designs remain as unusual and special examples of his body of work. Whereas countless other architects of his period designed from English, French, and Colonial antecedents, few worked from specific Scandinavian roots. Although some have thought that Lundie used a Scottish source for his ideas, his process of design suggests otherwise and that he made no attempt to search his ancestral origins in the evocation of his ideas. Rather he steadfastly clung to the rich training he received from his mentors and quoted sources for his designs that both he and his clients could believe in.

John Ruskin, the late nineteenth-century English essayist and architectural critic, stated that "no one can be a good architect who is not a metaphysician."[24] A metaphysician is someone versed in that division of philosophy that includes ontology, or the science of being, and cosmology, or the science of the fundamental causes and processes in things. Certainly it is unlikely that such terms ever crossed the lips of Lundie; nevertheless, the search for knowing about the making of things transforms his work so that the output is distinct from that of his colleagues and contemporaries. His work stands as testimony to a remarkable professional career.

NOTES

1. "In Conversation with Mr. Lundie," 106 (below).
2. "In Conversation with Mr. Lundie," 105 (below).
3. "Edwin Lundie, FAIA, Architect, 1886–1972," *Northwest Architect,* Mar.–Apr. 1972, p. 75.
4. "The Post-Modern House," *Architectural Record* 97 (May 1945): 70–75, reprinted in revised form in Joseph Hudnet, *Architecture and the Spirit of Man* (Cambridge: Harvard University Press, 1949), 108–19, and in Lewis Mumford, *Roots of Contemporary Architecture* (New York: Reinhold, 1952), 306–16.
5. "Edwin Lundie," 75.
6. The *esquisse* was used in the École des Beaux-Arts; Henry H. Saylor, *Dictionary of Architecture* (New York: John Wiley and Sons, 1967).
7. For more on Chamberlain, see Samuel N. A. Chamberlain, *Etched in Sunlight* (Boston: Boston Public Library, 1968).
8. Author's interviews with Louis Bramstedt and Frank Clark, Lundie's draftsmen.
9. "Edwin Lundie," 75.
10. C. Alexander et al., "Wings of Light" pattern II, in *Pattern Language* (Oxford: Oxford University Press, 1977).
11. This sketch is anonymous; if you can identify its author, please contact the publisher and credit will be given in future editions.
12. An obelisk is a shaft of square section and pyramidal tip, frequently tapering, usually commemorative; Saylor, *Dictionary of Architecture.*
13. A cartouche is a panel, tablet, or scroll, usually elaborated as a decorative spot, its plane or convex field sometimes bearing an inscription or date; frequently the cartouche interrupts or is imposed upon a molding. In *A Dictionary of Architecture and Building,* Russell Sturgis refers to cartouches also being done in wood or rectilinear form (New York: Macmillan Co., 1901).
14. The Arboretum was my introduction to Lundie; see Dale Mulfinger, "Edwin Lundie," *Architecture Minnesota,* Nov.–Dec. 1992, p. 50–51.
15. Dale Mulfinger, "Edwin Lundie: Architect with a Reliance on Type," in *Midgård: Type and the Possibilities of Convention* (Princeton: Princeton Architectural Press, 1991), 91–95.
16. Alan Colquhoun, "Typology and Design Method," in *Essays in Architectural Criticism: Modern Architecture and Historical Change* (Cambridge: MIT Press, Oppositions Books 1981), 43.

> Many people believe—not without reason—that the intuitive methods of design traditionally used by architects are incapable of dealing with the complexity of the problems to be solved and that without sharper tools of analysis and classification the designer tends to fall back on previous examples for the solution of new problems—on type solutions. . . . Thomas Maldonado admitted that in cases where it is not possible to classify

every observable activity in an architectural program, it might be necessary to use a typology of architectural forms in order to arrive at a solution. But he added that these forms were like a cancer in the body of the solution. . . . One of the most frequent arguments used against typological procedures in architecture has been that they are a vestige of an age of craft.

My purpose . . . is not to advocate a reversion to an architecture which accepts tradition unthinkingly. This would imply that there was a fixed and immutable relation between forms and meaning. The characteristic of our age is change, and it is precisely because this is so that it is necessary to investigate the part which modifications of type solutions play in relation to problems and solutions which are without precedent in any received tradition.

17. Stavra or stave construction technique is common to Norway and parts of Sweden; see Gunner Bugge and Christian Norberg-Schulz, *Stav Og Laft: Early Modern Architecture in Norway* (Oslo: Byggehurst-Norske Arkitekters Landsforbund, 1969).

18. Couple's realm is a nonsexist, more descriptive, term introduced here by the author but originated from *Pattern Language,* 648.

19. Note the comparison of Lundie chimney designs to those recorded in Chamberlain, *Etched in Sunlight,* or as recorded in his other text, *British Bouquet* (New York: Gournet Distributing Corp., 1963).

20. Saylor, *Dictionary of Architecture.*

21. *Pattern Language,* 641.

22. *Carl Larsson–Fifty Paintings* (Silver Spring, Md.: Nordic Heritage Service, Inc., 1985), 92.

23. Dale Mulfinger and Leffert Tigelaar, "Minnesota Lake Cabins," *Fine Homebuilding,* Spring 1993 (annual issue on houses), 59–61.

24. John Ruskin, *The Poetry of Architecture* (1893; New York: AMS Press, 1971).

0   6   12   18   24

Building plans are shown to a common scale
(as illustrated), except for the
Minnesota Landscape Arboretum.

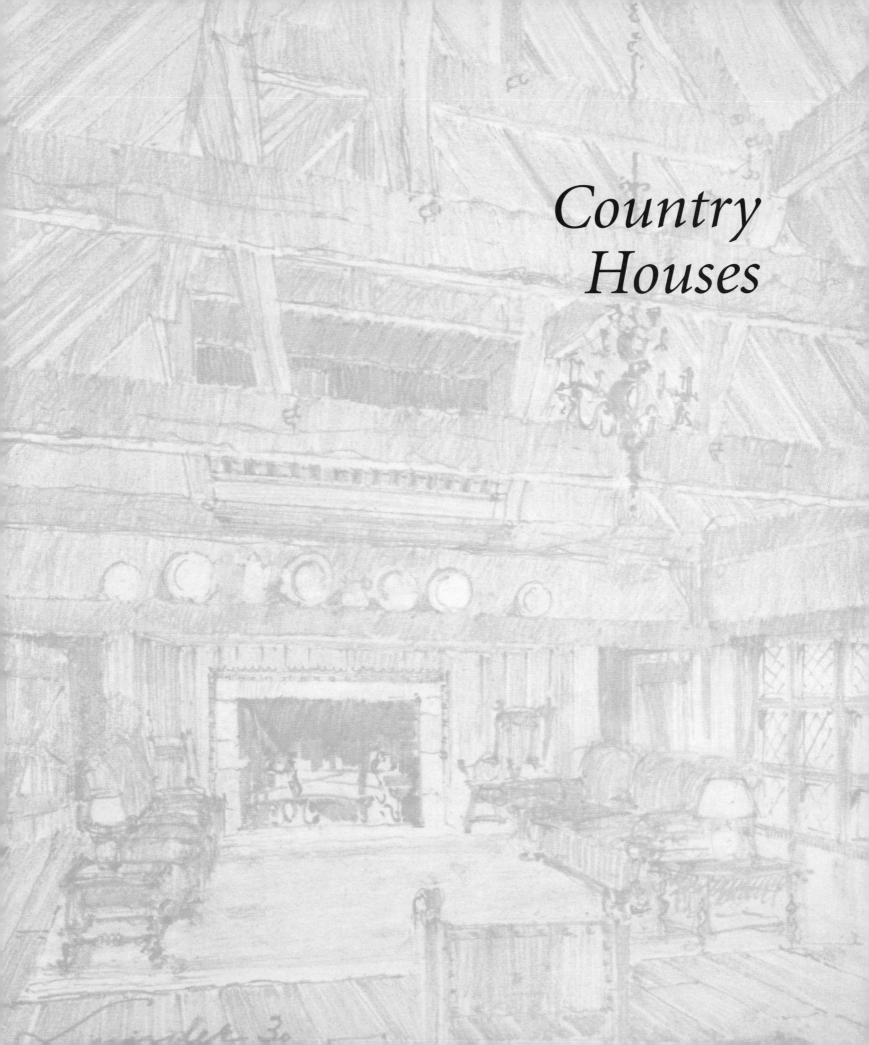

Country Houses

Daniels Estate

GEM LAKE
1930–36

Lundie designed the main house, the guest house, the service houses, and a barn, which included staff living quarters, for this estate. Originally called Worsted Skeynes, the estate was the project of Mrs. Daniels. Later, under the ownership of her son John, the guest house was enlarged to become the family's postwar home. By the 1980s individual families owned the different structures. The entry drive passes the service buildings and guest house before terminating in a loop in front of the main house. Until Lundie designed a dining room addition that formed a T plan, this was a long thin house with a varied roofscape. It is characterized by massive, highly sculpted, brick chimneys and a three-dormer configuration. The house ends with a small gable (couple's realm). The living room is a classic hall, which separates two second-floor wings of sleeping spaces. The house is richly detailed with elaborate custom-made wrought iron and millwork, leaded windows, and finish carpentry.

Front entry of the main house

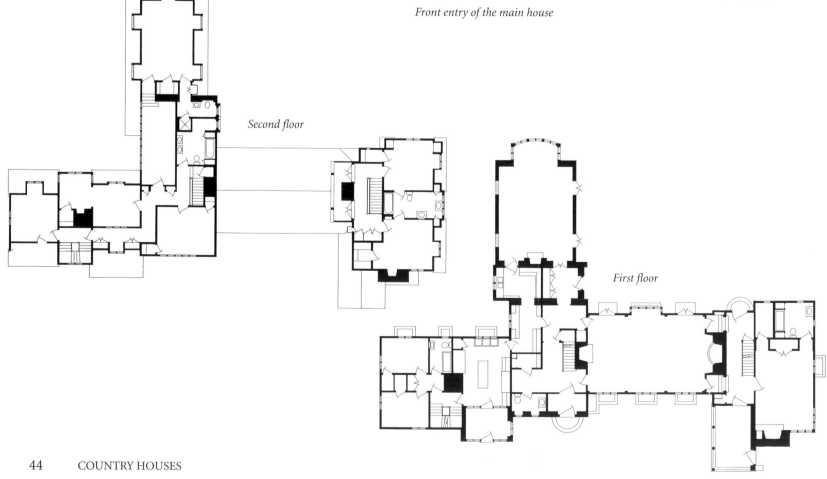

Second floor

First floor

Wrought-iron door knocker

The living room looking toward the east fireplace

A leaded-glass window

Guest house

Second floor of guest house

Fireplace in the guest house

First floor of guest house

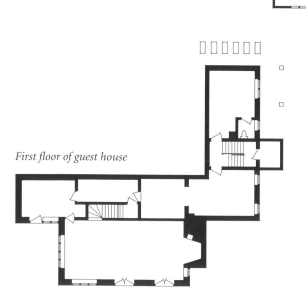

Doors and window of the barn

Front of the house, showing the dormers and the chimneys

Driscoll House

SUNFISH LAKE
1930–37 AND 1967–70

Lundie designed the original two-story, central Colonial portion of the present house for Dr. Frederick M. Owens in 1930-37 and later did the addition for the Driscolls. A pastoral drive leads through the wooded lakeside lot to the front of the house and ends in a circular return. The house consists of four connected forms: the garage, the main house, the angled addition, which is terminated with a small house shape, and the dining room, which is a perpendicular addition to the back of the original house. The garage colonnade provides interest and depth for the elevation, while subduing the garage image.

The original Colonial is divided on the ground floor into a living room and kitchen. The kitchen consists of many different parts, all incorporated into one space to become the family gathering area. One of the great aspects of this house is the curved hallways that connect the old house to the addition, emphasizing the deviation from the parallel in the plan. The custom-designed details are lavish in craftsmanship and numerous in quantity, such as the carefully composed lamppost on an asymmetrical base, curved bathroom door, curved vanity, and richly detailed wood plank floors.

The front of the house, facing the circular drive

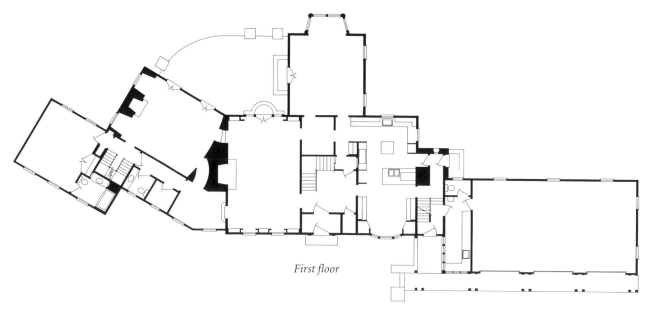

First floor

The front of the house, showing the "little house"

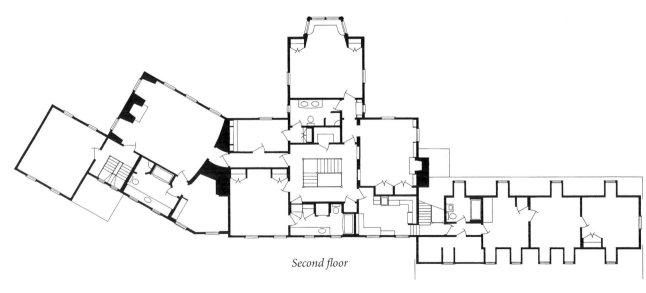

Second floor

The dining room bay

The curved door for the bathroom

Gainey Estate

OWATONNA
1960

Two big, stone entry pillars are evidence that this entrance drive leads to more than an ordinary residence. Just beyond the entry gate is the gate house, a small Colonial structure, as well as the horse stables and other service buildings. The main house is reached some distance beyond on a drive that winds through a beautifully planted, hilly landscape. The whitewashed brick exterior of the house evokes the spirit of the French-Provincial style and carries many interpretations and details specific to Lundie. A main, two-story gable form is the central connective piece for the smaller gables built around it. The house interior is also French in style and elegantly detailed. The bathrooms, for example, have custom-made, gold-plated faucets and light pink and gray marble. A burnished granite fireplace enhances the basement rathskeller.

The living room

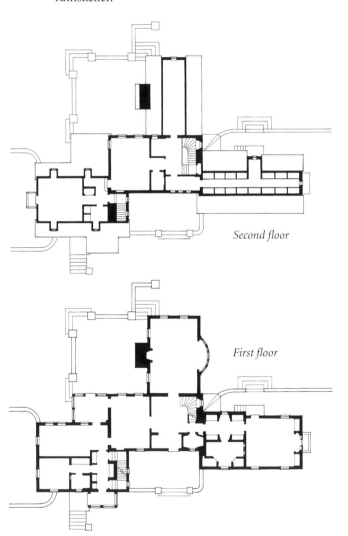

Second floor

First floor

The main house under construction

The main house, showing Lundie details on the dormers

A detail of the carved-wood ceiling in the living room

A bathroom with gold-plated fixtures

Little Estate

WINONA
1926

This large, seemingly misnamed, estate is located in slightly rolling countryside near Winona. It consists of a large country house, two separate garage structures, a guest house, which Lundie later remodeled, and other outbuildings. The sprawling, brick, Colonial-style house is an assemblage of connected, differently sized gable forms whose hierarchy relates to the program inside. The gable form in which the living room is located is the largest, stepping down gradually to the small forms that house the bedroom and kitchen. The interior is exquisite in its detailing and has many custom-designed and finely detailed doorknobs, latches, hinges, light fixtures, and millwork.

The main house as an assemblage of small structures (viewed from the south)

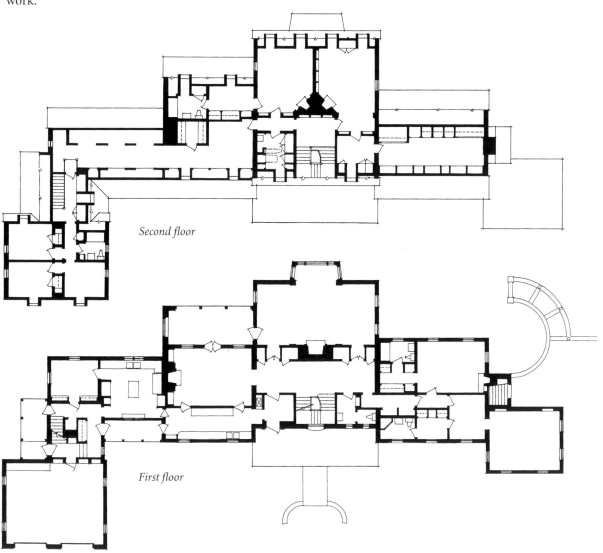

Second floor

First floor

Custom-made doorknob

Cabinet bin with wrought-iron hinge

The main house in its country setting

The guest house after Lundie remodeled the dormers

Side view of the bay

An outbuilding on the estate grounds

Large windows in the back of the house overlook the countryside.

COUNTRY HOUSES   57

Private Residence

SUNFISH LAKE
1938

When the owners of this property first approached Lundie, they showed him pictures of Cape Cod houses as photographed by Samuel Chamberlain. They wanted a Cape, but their program could not be accommodated within a single, gabled structure. The design that resulted was a house that appears to be a Cape that has been added onto. From certain vantage points in the pastoral yard, only the Cape image is visible. The front door thus becomes a seldom-used back door to the house, and the actual front entrance is at the joint of the Cape and the addition. Heavy timber construction characterizes the first floor. The rooms of the upper level are connected by a labyrinth of corridors and double doors.

The approach to the back of the house

Second floor

First floor

The dining room

The seldom-used front door

The Cape as viewed from the pastoral yard

Slade House

NORTH SHORE OF LAKE SUPERIOR
1940

This house presents itself in a modest way by projecting only the small vestibule toward the drive. Most of the house on the landward side is hidden from view because the site slopes steeply toward the lake. The entry separates the living and the sleeping areas of the house. The living spaces, consisting of a large hall on the second floor and a dining room directly below it, are set at an angle from the rest of the house and receive light from three sides. Two sides provide spectacular views of Lake Superior. The timber framing in these rooms sets the tone for the expression of the frame throughout the rest of the house. Many exquisitely crafted details fill the house, including custom-designed moldings, doors, light fixtures, latches, and wrought-iron hinges. Each room has its own motif developed with particular woods and hardware.

The landward side of the house showing the entry

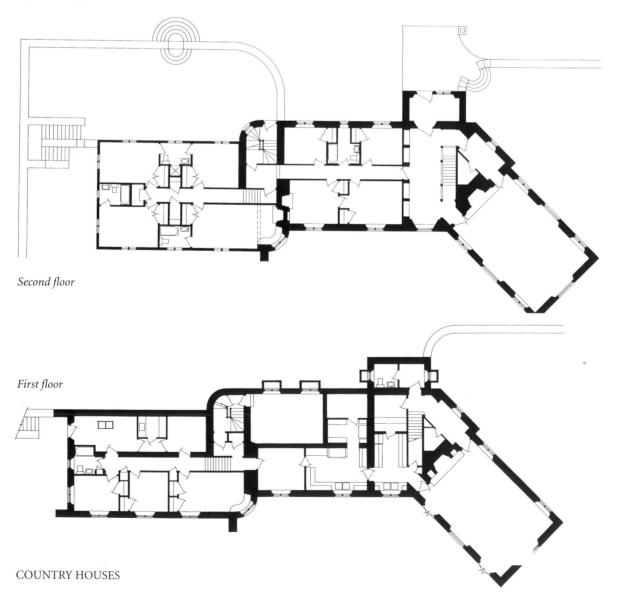

Second floor

First floor

The lakeside façade

Like other Lundie structures, this house fits its site well.

The latch, hinges, molding, and light fixture feature unusual detailing.

Dining room

A built-in bed in one of the bedrooms

Living room

Thompson Shooting Box

WINDOM
1940

The unique game of "bobble ball" was the starting point of this hunting-lodge design. The farmhouse that once stood on this spot was the basis upon which the Thompson family developed their game. After this house, which had a U-shaped plan, burned down, the family was adamant about replacing it with a structure that would replicate the game court. The result was the Shooting Box. The house is characterized by a large, hall-like vaulted living space that connects two one-and-a-half-story gabled wings. Curved queen posts in the timber-frame truss of the living room create a boatlike space overhead. The Shooting Box is an excellent example of Lundie's technique of scaling down the mass by dividing it into different gabled forms.

Connection detail where the living-room truss meets the wall

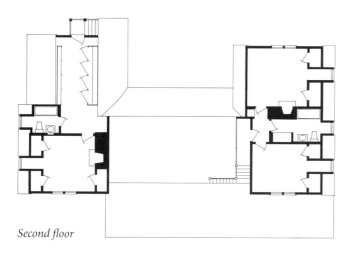

Second floor

The bar is partially tucked away under the stairway in the living room.

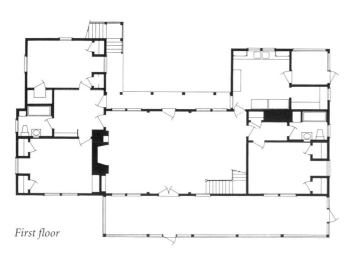

First floor

Carved wood adorns the fireplace.

The curved queen posts in the living room

The gabled wings of the house are joined by the vaulted living room.

Weyerhaeuser House

MANITOU ISLAND, WHITE BEAR LAKE
1926–31

This wood-shingled, rambling Colonial house is located on the tip of a promontory at the end of an island in White Bear Lake. This site provides a spectacular lake view, which was originally framed by a dock on one side and a guest house on the other. Guests arrived as often by boat as by car. (The guest house was later hauled across the ice to a site several miles inland on the other side of the lake.) A circular drive leads the guest through a porte-cochère, which marks the main entrance. The house is L shaped in plan and is one of Lundie's most dramatic examples of stepping down the form through diminished gable shapes. The stepping roof is emulated on the inside through level changes between rooms and in the corridors. The spectacular large chimney supplies three fireplaces with flues and also houses a circular stair that connects the main level to a tunnel leading to the dock.

Back of the house showing the porch

One of the carved post tops of the picket fence

Lantern near the front door

Doorknob on an interior door

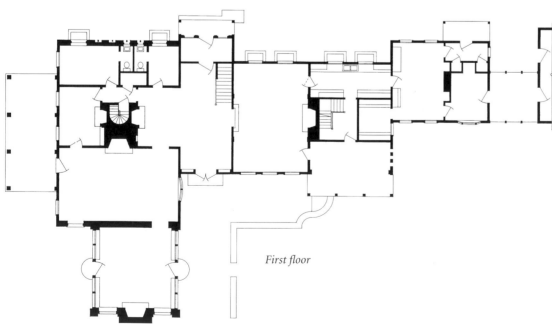

First floor

The garage wing of the house

Second floor

The lakeside view of the house

The front door, opening into the central hallway, has the dimensions Lundie often liked to use.

Interior of the porch

The dining room

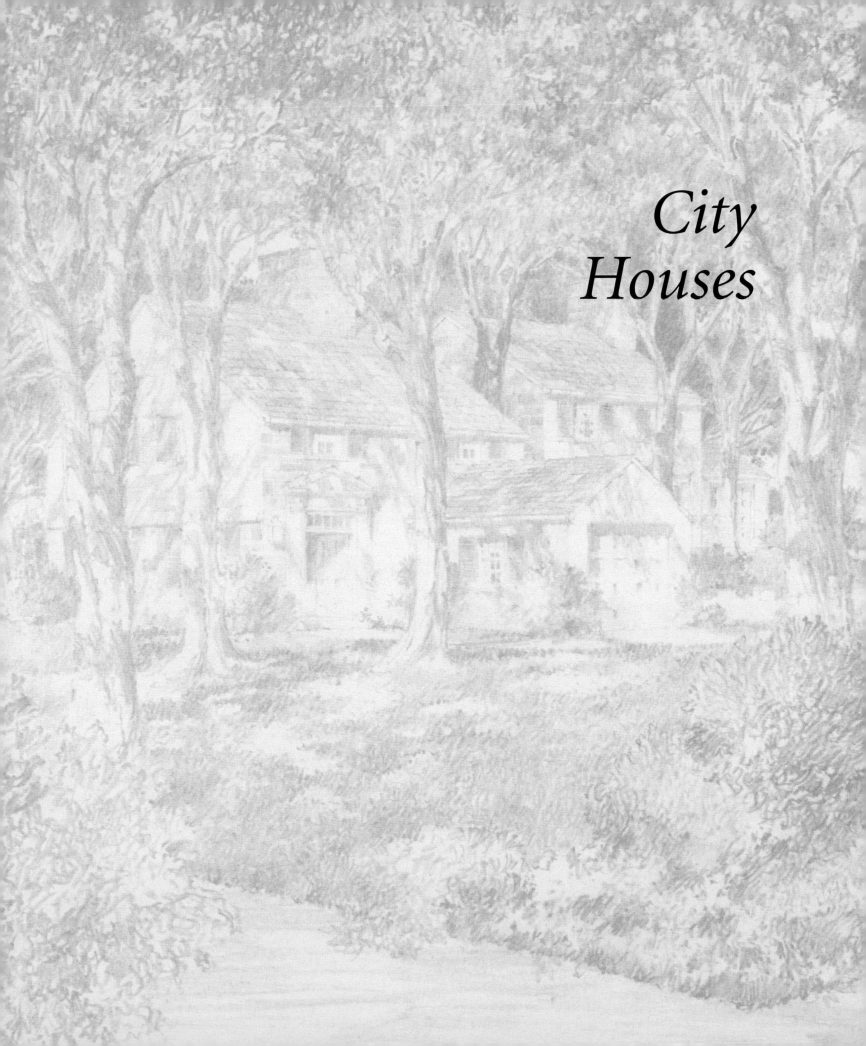

*City
Houses*

Aberle House

ST. PAUL
1927

This Cotswold-style house is located in the Crocus Hill neighborhood of St. Paul, overlooking the Mississippi River valley. The site is a rectangular corner lot, with narrow street face fronting the bluff. On the side of the house where it meets its neighbor, the house has few windows; the principal windows are oriented to the street and river valley. The house has multicolored lime-stone walls and a slate roof. In plan the house is basic-ally a Greek cross, where the stair and entry are located approximately at the meeting point of the arms of the cross. Characteristic of this house is the oriel window in the dining room and two traditionally detailed brick chimneys. On the interior, slight level changes between rooms suggest the steep grade between Crocus Hill and downtown St. Paul.

The corner entry to the house

The small dormer window seems to have a decorative rather than a functional purpose.

Eave detail

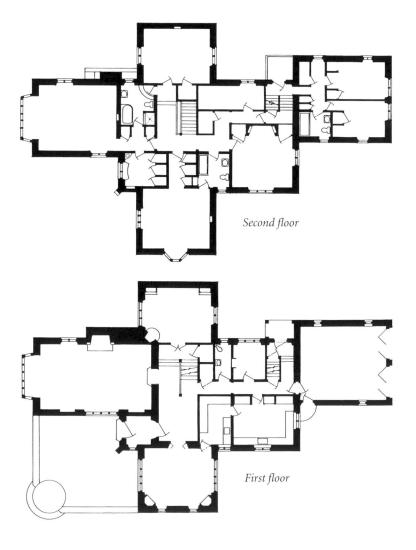

Second floor

First floor

Anderson House

MENDOTA HEIGHTS
1959

This house presents its Cape Cod image picturesquely to the suburban street on which it is located. Designed for two schoolteachers, this house exemplifies Lundie's concern for clients with modest budgets. Two joined, gabled, wood-shingle-covered forms, one for the main house and the other for the attached garage, reduce the mass of this small house to an even more intimate scale. The addition of shutters and muntined windows are further refinements of scale. The back of the house is articulated with dormers, bringing light to rooms at the roof level.

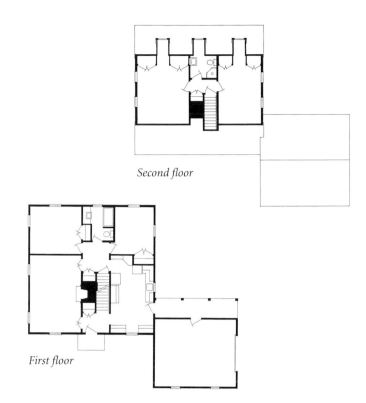

Second floor

First floor

The front façade of the house

Binswanger House

ST. PAUL
1926

This heavily rusticated, multicolored limestone house is situated on a bluff high above the Mississippi River in St. Paul. The lot has a quaint alley entrance to a European-style courtyard. The public rooms focus toward the river valley and sunny side of the lot. The house, designed about the same time as the Aberle residence, is in a detailed Cotswold style and has a similar corner entry into a T plan. The circulation hub lies at the intersection of the bars of the T, allowing the projecting rooms to have light on three sides. The house is characterized by its many gables, protruding eave lines, and such other features as an oriel window above the entry and idiosyncratic detailing on the rain leader.

The entry to the house from the cul-de-sac

Wrought-iron lantern at the front entrance

Lundie used both limestone and slate for the chimney.

Second floor

First floor

Delander House

ST. PAUL
1929–30

The two gable end walls are the bookends that embrace this large, formal, Georgian-style house. The thick walls contain the fireplace chimneys and also create deep window openings, deep enough to allow the interior shutters to disappear when opened against them. A formal, symmetrical façade directs the scale of the rooms and the classic, center-hall plan. The modern service element of this plan, anachronistic with a Georgian house, includes the kitchen, the maid's quarters, and the garage. It was designed as a one-story appendage to the rear of the house, to appear as if added at a later date.

An arched pediment, columnar molding, and leaded glass accent the entry.

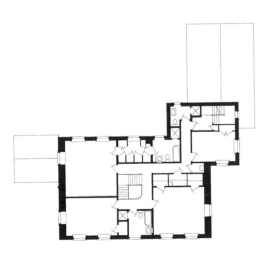

Second floor

First floor

The door to the porch

The back entry

Fiterman House

MINNEAPOLIS
1950–53

This large house is located near Lake of the Isles on a corner lot, which opens onto streets on the south and west (the lake) sides. The house consists of parallel units—a Cape Cod-style gabled roof and a garage gable, which are connected to each other by the dining room and a screened porch. The plan forms a square, enclosing an outdoor courtyard. The ground-floor, bedroom wing provides the south elevation with a small-scale gable and a massive, whitewashed brick chimney. This scheme successfully disguises the large footprint of the house in a village of forms reminiscent of French countryside cottages. A long organizing hallway connects entry, bedroom, and living spaces both inside and out. Many transition areas are formed through the use of thick walls, low ceilings, and closets between rooms. This house is richly detailed in both painted and stained moldings, cabinets, and mantels. Unusual metal hardware and lathed wood lanterns adorn this project, and a tray ceiling articulates the porch.

Exterior of the bedroom wing

The library, showing the thick walls

The bedroom corridor

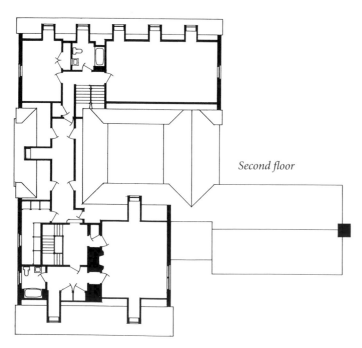

Second floor

First floor

The lakeside façade of the house

The back of the house, showing the garage

The kitchen with a built-in stove

The porch, looking toward the garage

Merritt House

ROCHESTER
1950–53

This quaint Colonial is located on a large corner lot in the "Pill Hill" neighborhood, overlooking the hospitals and Mayo Clinic in downtown Rochester. A rustic timber-framed, farmhouse-style kitchen forms the connecting piece between a traditional Cape Cod and the garage to create a house that is suitable for modern living without any loss of charm. To stay within their budget, the owners opted for a well-appointed but modest house. The result is a finely detailed house with many built-ins, traditionally applied multilayered paint finishes, and three fireplaces, of which the oversized brick hearth in the kitchen is especially memorable. Built-in storage, a frequent device of Lundie's, forms a break between the living room and the den.

The lantern at the front door

The hearth in the kitchen

The main façades of the house as it faces the corner

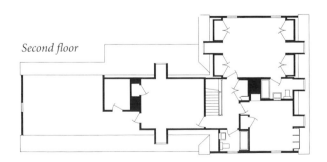

Second floor

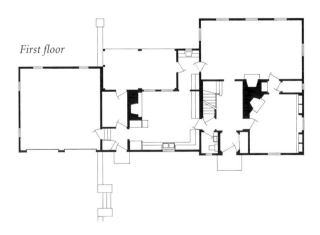

First floor

Rerat House

GOLDEN VALLEY
1954–56

This brick, French Provincial-style house is located on a cul-de-sac in a suburban setting just west of downtown Minneapolis. The L-shaped plan is split into sleeping and living wings. The living wing features a large fireplace that separates the dining and living rooms. The plan does not provide for servants' quarters, which indicates a shift from past values for those able to afford grand suburban residences in the 1950s. An eat-in kitchen with its own fireplace and a backyard fireplace just outside the kitchen give evidence of changing living requirements of post–World War II Americans. The beautifully detailed and weathered chimney reveals brickwork characteristic of Lundie designs. The inviting but formal entry faces south and provides a large rathskeller, which is below the living area, with an abundance of light. The courtyard is created in part by the shift in the library mass, which looks as if it were itself a small house. This technique of scaling a large house to look modest was one of Lundie's favorites, quite possibly gleaned from his books of French country houses.

The courtyard and front entry of the house

Rear entry and outdoor fireplace

Window detail

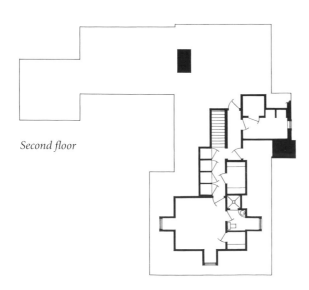

Second floor

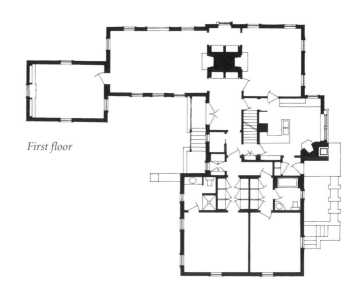

First floor

Spink House

ST. PAUL
1937–38

This shingle-clad Cape Cod is located on a small city lot. Unlike most of Lundie's houses, it is on a busy thoroughfare and has become wedged between two nondescript late-1960s apartment buildings. Small in scale, the house has finely detailed custom millwork, such as the Dutch entry door, and a charming brick fireplace. A tiny window in a second-floor bedroom provides a playful one-person view from a bed placed in that corner. The plan features a principal room for both living and dining, a diminutive version of the great halls of his larger house designs.

This house shows Lundie's use of gables for the main structure and the garage.

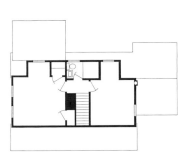

Second floor

First floor

The front door

The little window in the bedroom corner

The little window from the outside

Stakman House

ST. PAUL
1923–24

This house was one of Lundie's first residential designs. It has a traditional center-hall plan, but the massing of the house was adjusted to fit its sloping, triangular lot. The small gable of the screened porch presents the house to the street in a dignified but also humble manner. The front door, shutters, and other millwork details illustrate Lundie's interest early in his career in specific, highly detailed design.

Shutter with an urn-shaped, cut-out design

Columns and a curved pediment enhance the front door.

Stakman house front elevation

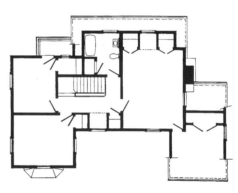

Second floor

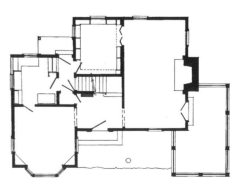

First floor

Weed House

WHITE BEAR LAKE
1939–40

This lakeside house was constructed with limestone that the owner salvaged from a building he demolished in downtown St. Paul. The formal, symmetrical façade seems wedged between the two heavy end walls and their chimneys. A wide front door invites a visitor into a home where the living and the outdoor spaces are focused toward the lake behind. Oversized, triple-hung windows emphasize the connection to the lake and transform this type of city house into a breezy and light lake home.

Detail showing how the old limestone fits around the new windows

The front of the house also features triple-hung windows.

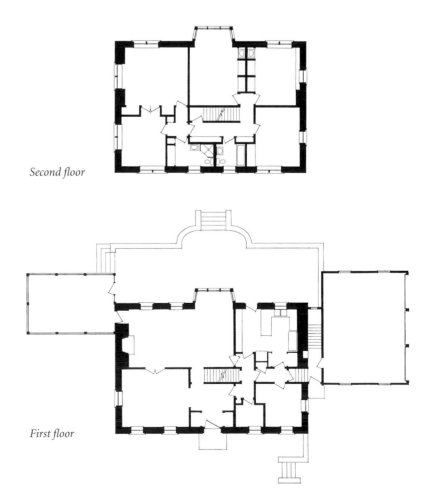

Second floor

First floor

Stocke House

ROCHESTER
1956–59

The mood of this house is French Provincial, mostly because of the clipped, hipped roof and the soft yellow hue of the brick exterior. The plan and form are neatly divided into three parts, each relating to a different segment of the program. The largest form, with a massive center chimney, represents the living space. The sleeping spaces are attached to the living space and shield it from the driveway approach. An entry court is formed by the strategic placement of a lamppost on an axis with the decorative brick gable above the front door. The solid timber frames that surround the windows have especially fine detailing.

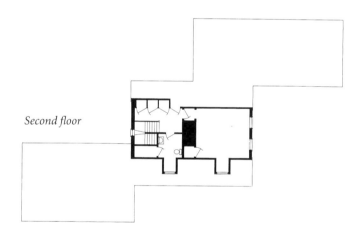

Second floor

First floor

The dormer windows that overlook the backyard

The top and bottom of the lamppost at the front entry

The living room window beneath the clipped, hip roof features carved trim.

The front entry and courtyard

Cabins

Clifford Cabin (Norcroft)

NORTH SHORE OF LAKE SUPERIOR
1947–49

The main mass of this gabled cabin is timber framed. An impressive girder truss transfers its load to a beam perpendicular to the fireplace. Although it is a strong expression of gravitational force, the precarious position of the beam above the hearth opening has more than once been the cause of a fire. The queen posts and tie beams determine the wall placement that divides the living room from other spaces on the main floor. The guest quarters above the attached garage are separate from the main cabin and are reached by an exterior stair. The pump house is a precursor of the transformer house that Lundie designed more than twenty years later at the Arboretum. A garage, work space, and a guest house are also a part of this retreat complex.

Exterior of the bedroom area, showing the timber framing and carved posts

The pump house

The living room features complex timber framing.

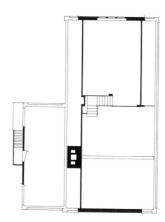

Second floor

First floor

Kromschroeder Cabin

NORTH SHORE OF LAKE SUPERIOR
1945–46

The simple plan of this cabin has basically remained as Lundie designed it, although some additions have been made. Because the site is inland from the shore, the cabin is not so directional in its window placement (toward the lake view) as the other Lundie cabins on the North Shore. The focus of the timber-frame gable is a large stone fireplace, which forms a division between the living space and the bedroom and kitchen. A sleeping loft above the bedroom and kitchen is reached by a ladder and provides an overlook into the living space below. The most striking features of this cabin are a few highly decorative and structural elements, such as the turned corner columns, the frame wedges, and the charming entrance canopy. The plans for this cabin are exquisitely simple yet meticulously organized.

Floor plan

Entry canopy at the front door

The cabin's main façade

Curtis Cabins

NORTH SHORE OF LAKE SUPERIOR
1946–49

This charming collection of four timber-framed structures is located on a long, thin lakeshore site, which was created by the placement of a large retaining wall on the steep slope toward the lake. Upon arrival, the visitor first sees the garage with guest quarters above it through the dense foliage of the site. The path then takes a sharp turn and leads to a small guest cabin with a huge stone chimney. This one-room cabin has built-in bunks, a galley kitchen hidden behind decorative scroll-cut doors, and a large corner fireplace. The terminus of the path is marked by the main cabin and a timber-framed woodshed. The large framed space of this cabin is divided at the points of the queen posts. This division determined the placement of the sculpted fireplace and the wall between the kitchen and living space. A long bank of divided-light windows creates a marked contrast of openness to the heavily grounded stone fireplace at the center.

Garage next to the retaining wall, overlooking the lake

The guest cabin

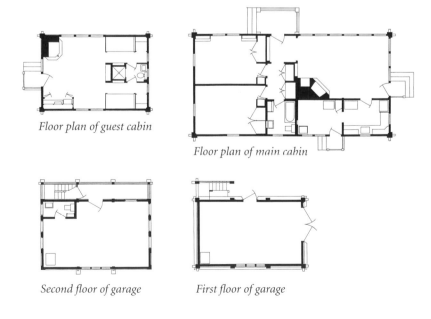

Floor plan of guest cabin

Floor plan of main cabin

Second floor of garage

First floor of garage

The covered entry of the main cabin

Corner post of the garage

Corner post of the main cabin

Windows with carved trim

Living room of the main cabin

Lundie designed the furniture for the garage guest quarters.

Corner post of the guest house

The garage, showing the exterior stairway on the lakeside

Door detail

The main cabin

Lundie Cabin

NORTH SHORE OF LAKE SUPERIOR
1941

This one-room cabin is the epitome of Marc-Antoine Langier's idea of primitive dwelling; man first builds a fire, then encloses a protective space around this source of warmth. The oversized chimney dominates Lundie's cabin and divides the one room into different realms—the living area is wedged between the place for cooking and the sleeping bunks. A large bank of windows opens the space toward the lake and south light. The turned and carved corner posts and hand-wrought hardware exemplify Lundie's love for well-crafted detail. (It also shows that he truly believed in what he designed for his clients; what was appropriate for his clients was good enough for him.) His plans included a separate gabled studio parallel to the main cabin and connected by an enclosed catwalk or hallway. He also suggested this improvement for the nearby Daniels cabin, but in neither case was the addition built.

The massive fireplace and chimney feature carefully crafted stonework.

Wrought-iron door hinge

The carved corner posts are a highlight of the cabin.

Floor plan

Stocke Cabin

TOFTE
1952

Stocke, a contractor from Rochester, built Lundie-designed houses in Rochester (including his own house), as well as the Gainey Estate in Owatonna. The cabin, perched on a promontory high above the lake, has spectacular vistas from two sides. Large picture windows provide a view along the shoreline, whereas a window seat looks out over Lake Superior. The house is divided into two gabled forms—the main cabin and a service area. The primary entrance is at the meeting point of the two forms. This is one of Lundie's later cabins in which the frame is expressed through specific use of siding material, rather than being exposed to the elements. Lundie also designed a separate detached garage.

Morning sunshine highlights the cabin's timber siding.

The window seat next to the fireplace also functions as a firewood storage chest.

Floor plan

The entrance porch

Olson Cabin

NORTH SHORE OF LAKE SUPERIOR
1948–51

A cantilevered, timber-framed front porch, reminiscent of those found on Alpine chalets, adorns this lakeside cabin. Aside from the balcony and dormers, an exquisite timber frame is protected by the single gable roof. A large living space opens up to the lake view through the continuous bank of windows, which is interrupted only by a large, stone corner fireplace. A trussed ridge beam orders the placement of the bedrooms below two sleeping lofts, which overlook the main living space. The timber-framed roof construction emphasizes the ridge beam and the queen posts by exaggerating their size. The tie beams subtly define the separation among activities within the living space.

Cabin interior showing the timber-frame construction

Second floor

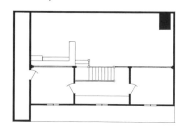

First floor

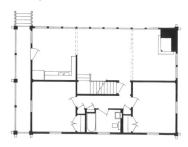

Casement window and downspout

The cabin features a carved corner post on the porch and details on the dormers

Wrought-iron door latch

Wrought-iron cabinet hinge

Robinson Cabin

NORTH SHORE OF LAKE SUPERIOR
1957–58

This house has a friendly expression that is achieved by its clean white appearance, the welcoming entry porch, and the wonderful scale of the three shed dormers. It is part of a second generation of Lundie timber-frame cabins in which the timber frame, to avoid deterioration through exposure to the elements, is covered completely by wood siding. Although the frame is concealed, the rusticated siding provides the outlines that hint at the frame. Every element inside of this cabin, except for the furniture, was specifically designed by Lundie and custom built by local craftsmen. This detailed work includes decorative brickwork on the massive fireplace and chimney and the pulpitlike stair landing that projects into the living space. The frame in the living space is richly carved, and some members are held together by large, decoratively cut wedges.

The stairway and landing

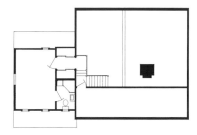

Second floor

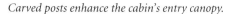

Carved posts enhance the cabin's entry canopy.

First floor

The cabin fits comfortably into its lakeside setting.

Detail of the textured post

Detail of the eaves

The living area features elaborate brickwork and carving.

Weyerhaeuser Cabin

BRULE RIVER, WISCONSIN
1966–72

This cabin complex consists of three buildings: a main cabin, a guest cabin, and a garage. As one of Lundie's late works, it shows how he manipulated the timber frame to create space, form window openings, and provide "a timber frame vocabulary" for the exterior cladding. Although the cabin does not expose the frame to the exterior, the logic of the frame is clearly readable through the configurations of siding materials. These elements are part of Lundie's regionalistic vocabulary. The living and kitchen spaces in the main cabin are separated by a large chimney. It provides the living room with a large hearth and the kitchen with a place for the ovens and barbecue. In the living space the frame divides the wall plane horizontally, creating a lower band of large windows and a smaller strip above of clerestory windows. The frame also forms the railing of the second-floor landing. The guest cabin's squared-off logs are fancifully carved and cantilevered to create a covered entry porch. An unusual timber-frame porch, expressive of the trees surrounding it, adorns the river side of this cabin.

The main cabin

Second floor

First floor

Detail of the main cabin timber siding

The guest cabin porch

The timber framing in the main cabin living room

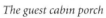

The garage

Detail of the front door

Other Structures

38

Minnesota Landscape Arboretum

CHANHASSEN
1966–72

This is the only Lundie building open to the public aside from Lutsen Resort. The Arboretum, owned and operated by the University of Minnesota, consists of gardens, groves, and a collection of buildings set in a gently undulating landscape. The form of the main building was derived from a much smaller unbuilt country house scheme, done in the 1930s. The disparate but connected gable forms, clad in wood and brick, visually divide the mass of this large building and step rhythmically into the land-scape. They give the appearance of a structure that has been accreted over time. The Y plan has an entry near its center, separating the public wings from the office area. Connected to the massing are several exterior spaces: an outdoor entry room, a veranda for outdoor dining, and a patio to the south from which to begin touring. The wood-panelled hall is both the entry to the building, which includes a spectacular timber-framed library and the large fireplace room, as well as a gate to the gardens and groves beyond. The library and fireplace rooms are especially worth a visit, as they represent typical, well-detailed, and decorative Lundie-style timber framing. The light fixture in the fireplace room is made of lathe-turned wood. In the Arboretum gardens beyond the building is a timber-frame shelter, a gazebo in the rose garden, and a finely detailed well house. The Arboretum was Lundie's final commission and not fully realized before ill health terminated his involvement in the project.

The round patio showing the brickwork and wood siding

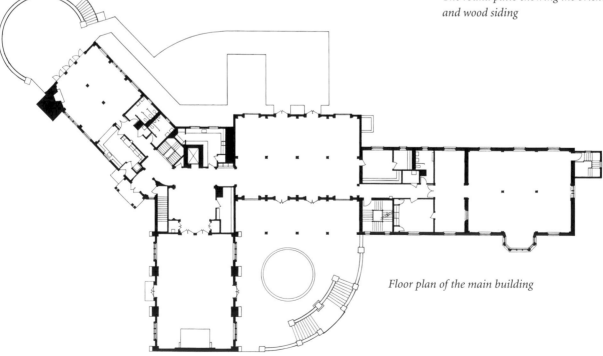

Floor plan of the main building

The front façade of the main building, with additions made to Lundie's orginal design

The entry porch

The many hanging lamps feature turned wood.

A column in the main hall

The rear façade of the main building

A window with cartouche above it

A small shelter on the Arboretum grounds

The pump house has carved wood and wrought iron.

Detail of carved wedges used on the pump house

A wooden fence encloses part of the grounds.

Lutsen Resort

LUTSEN
1949–60

A large obelisklike post that extends the Lutsen sign toward Highway 61 marks the location of this resort on the North Shore of Lake Superior. Lundie's plans for this lodge were built twice, as the original structure was tragically burned shortly after its construction. The newer version was expanded to include a swimming pool. Lundie also designed a roofed timber-frame bridge, which spans an adjacent stream, and many smaller cabins that were never built. The entry porch attached to the large, gabled main building extends a welcome to guests arriving at the lodge and lures them into a wood-panelled lobby and dining room. The lobby's great fireplace and flanking windows are spanned by an oversized carved beam. The stair that leads to the guest rooms upstairs shows Lundie's attention to minute details in the way the spindles are connected to the handrail and the treads to the stringers. Lundie often reflected the timber-frame look in the exteriors of structures by arranging the exterior sheathing material in a rich array of directions. Lutsen's broad lakeside façade exemplifies this detail.

The sign post near the highway

The main façade of the lodge faces the lake, which is off to the right.

The lobby stairway

Detail of the lobby stairway

Detail of wood carving

This covered bridge features carved posts.

Park Shelter

ST. PAUL
1926

This shelter is in Cochran Memorial Park on Summit Avenue in the Ramsey Hill neighborhood. This small, gabled structure is open to one side. The U-shaped stone wall that remains is symbolic of embrace, the essence of a shelter.

Detail of the stonework

The shelter faces a small, fenced pool. The statue is Indian Hunter and His Dog *(1926) by St. Paul native Paul Manship (1885-1966).*

In Conversation
with Mr. Lundie

First published in *Northwest Architect,* May–June 1969.

Northwest Architect: What influence did Cass Gilbert have on you as a person and as an architect?

Mr. Lundie: Application and lots of hard work in anything that you do—that, I believe, is the most profound influence he had on me and so strong that it is still with me to this day. It shaped my attitude and my entire outlook toward my work.

Q: When you started in the field of architecture, there weren't many schools?

Mr. Lundie: There were very few: Columbia, MIT, I'm not too sure but it may have been the University of Pennsylvania, but I don't think there were over those three. Everybody who started out in architecture at that time had to go the route that I did; it was about the pattern of that day. Can I boast a little? . . . I don't believe, honestly I don't believe, that I could ever have had the education in school, indoctrination and education in design and architecture such as I had from these three men. (Cass Gilbert, Thomas Holyoke and Emmanuel Louis Masqueray.) I don't think you would have found those men now on the staff at the teaching level.

Q: Your drawings and your pencil sketches are so beautiful. Can you tell us how you developed this talent? Did it come naturally?

Mr. Lundie: Yes, I think it did. We worked in those days until noon on Saturdays. I started out and probably my first effort was more in water color. I'd go home at noon on Saturday and start in first with water color and I'd work through Saturday afternoon and Sunday and then Sunday night I'd throw the whole thing in the waste basket and the next week I'd repeat. This went on and on and on. I suppose in the office I started doodling more with black and white, with pen. Masqueray used to encourage it, I mean if you did it. I remember the cathedral in Sioux Falls, I had the whole front elevation of that done just in pen and ink. It wasn't a show drawing, we didn't think of it that way, it was just studying detail as I went on later. But I think I started to fumble with it that way with black and white. Then I finally concluded after I got into practice myself and time was pretty precious, I would find that pen and ink was pretty laborious. It was hard to find the time to do what you really felt you should do, so then I began to experiment with pencil drawings. The reason I got into black and white at all was that you couldn't do water color very well at night. I love to draw and I suppose that's in back of the whole thing; I always love to draw.

Q: You were published in the *Architectural Record?*

Mr. Lundie: Russell Whitehead chose a group of things that he printed when he was on the staff of the *Record* that was nice. That came from a group of young architects in Saint Paul, they knew me, no one else outside knew me very well. One man had a little luncheon that noon for Russell Whitehead and he invited these young fellows to come in. I wasn't even known. Afterwards they came down to the office and brought Whitehead with them. These are the things that went on that I think were so nice when I speak of esprit de corps. Now here was a younger group, my generation, coming along with the same sort of feeling. They wanted him to see what I was doing, so that's how those things happened to be published.

Q: Mr. Lundie, you have a very special clientele?

Mr. Lundie: Well, I'm going to make a statement that I've made to myself all the time and I'm quite convinced that it's true, too, that I have always believed and always wished to attract through the performance of the office these people that I'm going to call the people who represent an *aristocracy of good taste.* I've no reason to change my mind. I think it comes from different levels; I have found that to be true. I found that it has an application for the bigger things that I've done. I find that it surely has an application for some of the littler things that I've done. There are people who I think have an awareness and appreciation for fine things and they want things done for them in the spirit of fine things within what they can afford to do.

Q: When you speak of fine things, specifically what do you have in mind?

Mr. Lundie: Everything. I'm talking about those things that go into making this their home, their surroundings in that house, everything that goes to make up their way of life in there I think is of great importance to them within their means.

Q: You've had clientele of the third generation.

Mr. Lundie: Yes, I have now the third generation of some of these families. My clients today are not very different from their parents and their grandparents in their appreciation and their knowledge of fine things. It's a tradition with them. I think it's a matter of feeling with them and it goes on and on.

Q: Mr. Lundie, as a student still in college, what advice would you give me?

Mr. Lundie: I don't know if I would dare. I think dedication and very hard work. I think I've worked two lifetimes and I'm not feeling sorry for myself. I do it because I enjoy it.

Q: Would you ever retire from architecture?

Mr. Lundie: I hope not. I hope when I fail to produce the way I think I should I'll be aware of it. I hope to be smart enough to step aside at that point.

Q: What do you think about the 65 retirement?

Mr. Lundie: I went by that long ago. I see a few cases and I feel awfully sorry for those men. It wouldn't interest me at all.

Q: You're doing the arboretum for the university?

Mr. Lundie: I have been doing all architectural design at the U of M landscape arboretum. I'm working on the center building out there now. All of this has been a great pleasure for me. To be associated with something that is all building up and not tearing down. We didn't destroy anything out there. I don't think we've cut down a tree yet.

Q: You've always had a small office, too?

Mr. Lundie: Yes, I've never had over three or four, maybe five at the most.

Q: You're on the boards yourself all the time aren't you?

Mr. Lundie: Oh, yes. I wouldn't know any other way to do it. I wouldn't want to sit in there and try to delegate it to someone else; I don't think I could, I don't think I'd know how and I like to get into it myself. Can a painter or portraitist paint the ears and then have an assistant paint the eyes and some other features? What do you suppose would happen and come out of this composite effort? I told you earlier about Masqueray; when he was working on water colors and somebody came in the office, looked at what he was doing and said, "Well, you're quite an artist." His answer was, "I wouldn't be an architect if I wasn't an artist."

Q: An architect also has to have a pretty good poetic sense, don't you think?

Mr. Lundie: I would call it imagination. I think I attribute my enjoyment in this profession to the fact that my grandparents and my parents fed me all of the romantic fiction of that age which was good. It was a high order of thing, it was very imaginative, I think sometimes to the point of exaggeration, and I think that's been true with me in my Architecture. You can always land with a dull thud if you have gotten up there in the clouds too far. I remember this sculptor friend of mine who always said, when he was making a portrait bust, in order to make a good portrait, a true portrait of that individual, there had to be an exaggeration of certain facial characteristics: the bone structure, contours and that sort of thing. It even had to be exaggerated to make it seemingly a true portrait. I think sometimes with architectural design you almost have to exaggerate some of it. I think mastery of *line* and *mass* and scale and proportion is important; it is part of the working tool. Knowledge of the materials and the crafts you're working is infinitely important. We're talking about design detail now and there are certain attributes of materials that call for different treatments, of doing things much finer, on a finer scale with some than with others.

Q: Do you ever wish that you would have practiced architecture in some other city?

Mr. Lundie: No, I could have gone to New York with Mr. Gilbert. He offered me a place in his office out there to come up with the crowd. Someone tried to get me to go to Chicago once to quite a nice office. Can I tell you a story about that? I got to the point of starvation once and I put a bundle of these drawings under my arm and went to Chicago. I thought maybe I could find architects down there who could use me; I could stay here; I could render their drawings; I could get a little income out of that. Everywhere I went I never had any trouble getting past the front foyer. They'd pick up the drawings and go into a private office and the next thing I knew I was in there along with the drawings. Usually the case was they wanted me to stay and that I didn't want. I thought, well, if anybody is interested in it, it may work out all right after all. I came back home and it wasn't long before something came. There was income again.

Q: Where do you think architecture is going?

Mr. Lundie: Well, that I don't know. I've got all I can do to keep my eye on what I'm doing here and do it just as well as I know how and let the rest of the world go by until it finally finds a resting place.

Lundie Project Timeline

The projects included in this timeline are ones for which Lundie did renderings. They are primarily, but not exclusively, residences. The information is based on drawings, records, and other materials in the Lundie Papers.

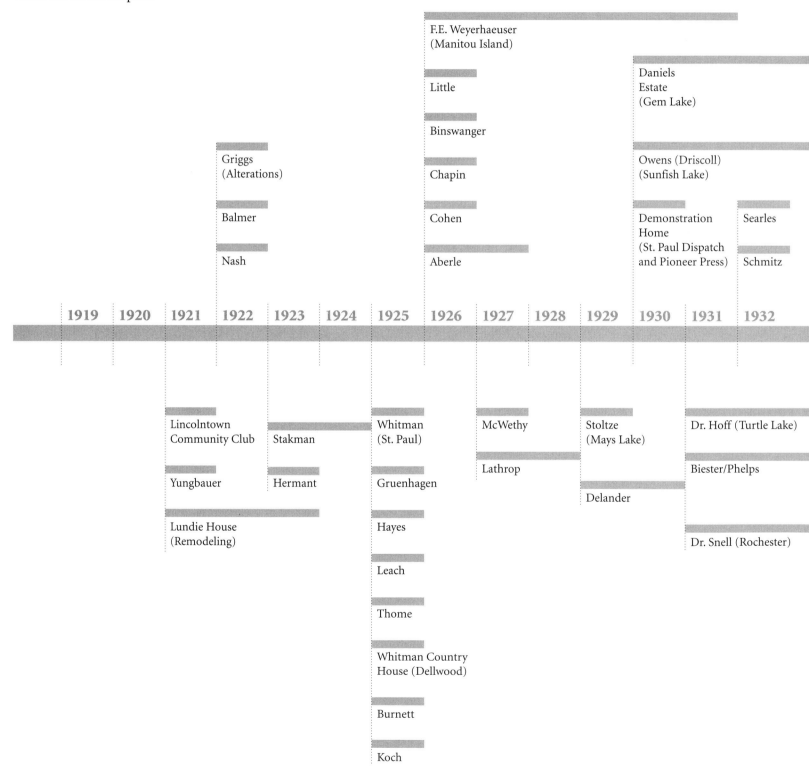

F.E. Weyerhaeuser
(Manitou Island)

Little

Binswanger

Chapin

Cohen

Aberle

Griggs
(Alterations)

Balmer

Nash

Daniels
Estate
(Gem Lake)

Owens (Driscoll)
(Sunfish Lake)

Demonstration
Home
(St. Paul Dispatch
and Pioneer Press)

Searles

Schmitz

| 1919 | 1920 | 1921 | 1922 | 1923 | 1924 | 1925 | 1926 | 1927 | 1928 | 1929 | 1930 | 1931 | 1932 |

Lincolntown
Community Club

Yungbauer

Lundie House
(Remodeling)

Stakman

Hermant

Whitman
(St. Paul)

Gruenhagen

Hayes

Leach

Thome

Whitman Country
House (Dellwood)

Burnett

Koch

McWethy

Lathrop

Stoltze
(Mays Lake)

Delander

Dr. Hoff (Turtle Lake)

Biester/Phelps

Dr. Snell (Rochester)

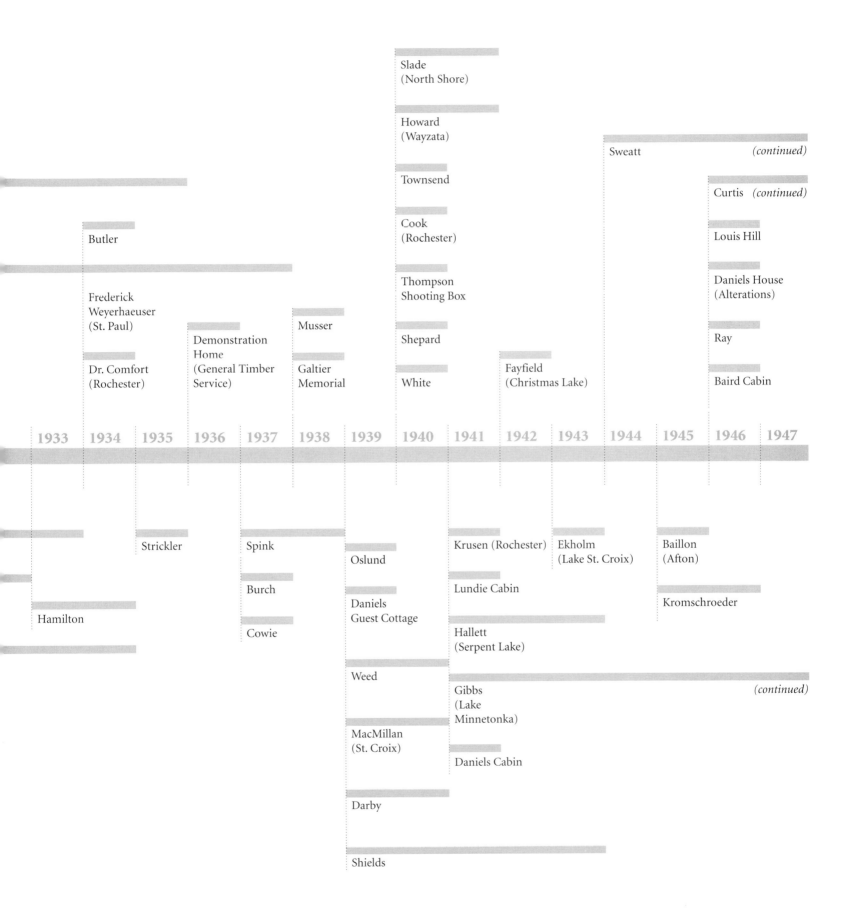

Slade
(North Shore)

Howard
(Wayzata)

Sweatt   *(continued)*

Townsend

Curtis   *(continued)*

Butler

Cook
(Rochester)

Louis Hill

Frederick
Weyerhaeuser
(St. Paul)

Thompson
Shooting Box

Daniels House
(Alterations)

Musser

Demonstration
Home
(General Timber
Service)

Shepard

Ray

Dr. Comfort
(Rochester)

Galtier
Memorial

White

Fayfield
(Christmas Lake)

Baird Cabin

1933 1934 1935 1936 1937 1938 1939 1940 1941 1942 1943 1944 1945 1946 1947

Strickler

Spink

Krusen (Rochester)

Ekholm
(Lake St. Croix)

Baillon
(Afton)

Oslund

Burch

Lundie Cabin

Kromschroeder

Hamilton

Daniels
Guest Cottage

Cowie

Hallett
(Serpent Lake)

Weed

Gibbs
(Lake
Minnetonka)   *(continued)*

MacMillan
(St. Croix)

Daniels Cabin

Darby

Shields

Olson

Bockstruck

McDonald

Fiterman

(Sweatt continued)

Merritt

(Curtis continued)

Voss
(St. James)

Dayton
(Minnetonka)

Stocke House
(Rochester)

Winters
(Dellwood)

Malone
(Windom)

Arboretum

Anderson

Foss (Rochester)

Bowman

Brewster

Rerat

Zalk (Duluth)

Love

Hunt

Bell

Fusfield
(Sioux Falls,
S. Dak.)

J.P. Weyerhaeuser
(Dellwood)

Sweatt
(Florida)

Ravlin

Stocke Cabin

Bros (Orono)

Gainey

| 1947 | 1948 | 1949 | 1950 | 1951 | 1952 | 1953 | 1954 | 1955 | 1956 | 1957 | 1958 | 1959 | 1960 |

Gainey

Carlson

Ebin

Arny

Robinson

Miller

Lutsen

(Gibbs continued)

Dr. Ferris
(Rochester)

Clifford

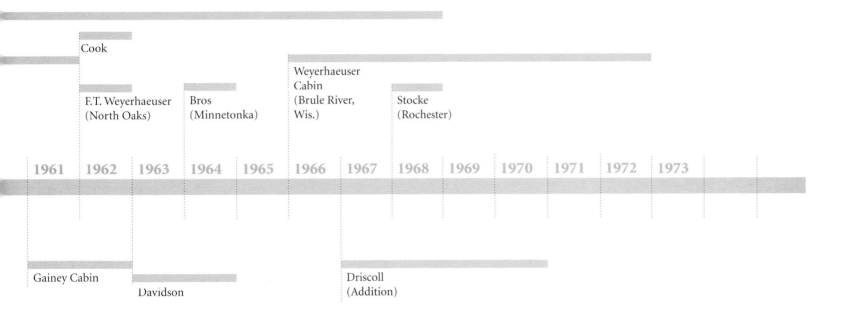

Cook

Weyerhaeuser
Cabin
(Brule River,
Wis.)

F.T. Weyerhaeuser
(North Oaks)

Bros
(Minnetonka)

Stocke
(Rochester)

| 1961 | 1962 | 1963 | 1964 | 1965 | 1966 | 1967 | 1968 | 1969 | 1970 | 1971 | 1972 | 1973 |

Gainey Cabin

Davidson

Driscoll
(Addition)

Index

Picture Credits

Perspective renderings in pencil on part-title pages include:

Edwin Lundie, p. 1: MacMillan house, Marine on the St. Croix

Edwin Lundie's Designs, p. 25: Garage, Weyerhaeuser house, Manitou Island, White Bear Lake

Country Houses, p. 43: Living room, Daniels estate, Gem Lake

City Houses, p. 71: Project for a group of houses, Bayard Avenue, St. Paul

Cabins, p. 87: Relocated Finnish cabin at Daniels cabin grounds, Schroeder

Other Structures, p. 103: Galtier Memorial, St. Paul

Photographs and other illustrations used in this book appear through the courtesy of the institutions or persons listed below. The name of the photographer, when known, is given in parentheses.

Minnesota Historical Society collections, St. Paul—pages 9 (Dennis Magnuson, *St. Paul Dispatch,* May 14, 1969, p. 25), 12, 15

Edwin H. Lundie Papers, Northwest Architectural Archives, University of Minnesota Libraries, St. Paul—pages 1, 3, 4, 5, 6, 7, 8, 11, 13, 14, 16, 18, 20 (top), 21, 25, 26, 33 (middle), 38 (top left), 43, 71, 87, 103.

Minnesota Society of American Institute of Architects—page 21 (right, *Northwest Architect,* May-June 1969, p. 20)

All remaining photographs are from private collections. Peter Kerze was the photographer for the pictures on pages 27, 32, 33 (bottom), 35 (top), 38 (top right), 44, 45 (left), 46 (top), 47, 48, 49, 50, 51 (bottom), 53 (top), 54, 55 (top left and bottom left), 56, 57, 58, 59, 60, 61 (top right and bottom), 62, 63, 65 (bottom), 67, 68, 69 (bottom), 72 (top), 74 (top), 75 (top), 77 (top and middle), 78 (bottom), 79, 80 (top), 82 (bottom), 83 (top), 84 (top), 85, 88 (top left and bottom), 89 (bottom), 90 (top), 87 (top), 88 (top), 93 (top right and bottom right), 90 (top), 95 (top), 96, 97 (top), 98, 99 (top right and bottom right), 108, 109, 110.

Dale Mulfinger was the photographer for the pictures on pages 33 (top), 34,. 35 (bottom), 36, 37, 38 (bottom), 39, 45 (right top and bottom), 46 (bottom), 51 (top), 52 (top), 53 (bottom left and bottom right), 55 (top right), 61 (top left), 64, 65 (top left and top right), 66, 69 (top), 72 (bottom), 73, 74 (bottom), 75 (bottom), 76, 77 bottom left and bottom right), 78 (top), 80 (bottom left and bottom right), 81, 82 (top left and top right), 83 (bottom), 84 bottom left and bottom right), 88 (top right), 89 (top), 90 (bottom), 87 (bottom left, bottom middle, and bottom right), 88 (bottom), 93 (top left and bottom left), 90 (middle and bottom), 95 (bottom left and bottom right), 97 (bottom left and bottom right), 99 (bottom left and bottom middle), 100, 101, 104, 105, 106, 107.

The photographer for the pictures on pages 31 and 52 was Grace (Mrs. Edwin) Lundie.

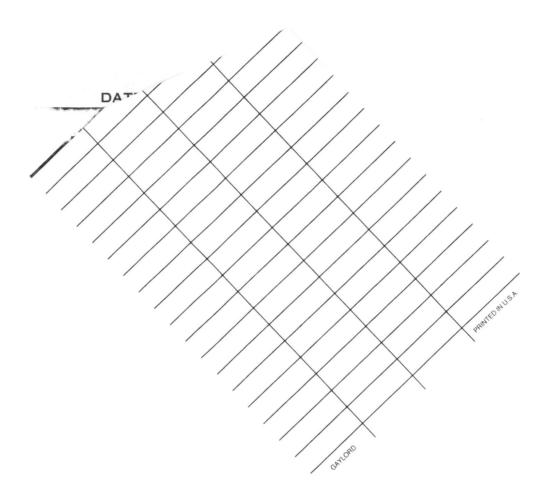

DAT

GAYLORD

PRINTED IN U.S.A.